HEMINGWAY'S KEY WEST

❖

HEMINGWAY'S KEY WEST

by
Stuart B. McIver

Pineapple Press, Inc.
Sarasota, Florida

Pineapple Press, Inc.
P.O. Drawer 16008
Southside Station
Sarasota, Florida 34239

LIBRARY OF CONGRESS CATALOGING-IN-PUBLICATION DATA
McIver, Stuart B.
Hemingway's Key West / by Stuart McIver
p. cm.
Includes bibliographical references and index
ISBN 1-56164-035-2
1. Hemingway, Ernest, 1899-1961—Homes and haunts—Florida—Key West. 2. Novelists, American—20th Century—Biography. 3. Literary landmarks—Florida—Key West. 4. Key West (Fla.)—Guidebooks 1. Title
PS3515.B37Z74117 1993
813'.52—dc20
(B) 93-14668
CIP

10 9 8 7 6 5 4 3 2

Design and composition by Robert Fleury

Printed and bound by Walsworth Company, Marceline, Missouri

To Joan, who came up with the idea,
and to my Uncle Bob

ACKNOWLEDGMENTS

Many people deserve thanks for their insight, information and encouragement, among them: Michael Whalton, Betty Bruce, Tom Hambright, Ruth Chados, Jim Plath, Sylvia Robards, Wright and Joan Langley, Lorian Hemingway, Hilary Hemingway Freundlich, John Boisonault, Arthur Valladares, Rosemary Jones, Jean Trebbi, Molly Wylly, Edmund and Carol Sadowski, and John Klausing.

TABLE OF CONTENTS

HEMINGWAY'S KEY WEST

CHAPTER I

❖ ❖ ❖ ❖ ❖ ❖ ❖ ❖ ❖ ❖ ❖

BONE KEY

JUST THE PLACE for "Ole Hem...to dry out his bones." That was the recommendation John Dos Passos made to fellow-novelist Ernest Hemingway. And, in fact, Hemingway's bones could use a good drying out. He had spent another cold, wet winter in his apartment on Paris's Left Bank.

Key West was a perfect choice for a man with cold bones. The island had once been called Cayo Hueso, Spanish for Bone Key. It was supposedly the site of an ancient Indian massacre that left its sands covered with sun-bleached skeletons. The bones had long ago been cleared out but part of the name stuck. Cayo Hueso was Anglicized into Key West.

The southernmost city in the United States, Key West was well-placed to pour on all the heat the author could stand. It missed being a tropical island by less than a hundred miles, a whim of geography that did little to compromise the key's Caribbean spirit—laid-back, relaxed, tolerant.

In every sense, Key West, some seven thousand miles to the southwest of Paris, was a far cry from the French metropolis–and not just in distance. By the 1920s the cosmopolitan French metropolis had become the artistic and intellectual capital of the world, home of Picasso, Chagall, Dali, cubism, Art Deco, Dada, the Ballet Russe, Nijinksy, Pavlova, *le jazz hot*, Coco Chanel, James Joyce, Gertrude Stein and, not incidentally, Ernest Hemingway.

Key West was, by contrast, a mess. By 1928 its population had shrunk from twenty-six thousand to ten thousand. Jobs were moving away as fast as a hooked tarpon's run. A blight wiped out the sponge industry. The Cuban cigar industry moved away to Tampa, leaving little but the rhythms of Spanish speech and the aroma of black bean soup. With onions. Conchs, a title reserved for Key West natives, eked out a living by fishing commercially or by smuggling booze from Havana. No wonder Ernest dubbed the town "the St. Tropez of the poor."

Key West had no literary, no artistic, no intellectual life. Hemingway would change that. The island the expatriate writer had planned to visit as a vacation hideaway would become the only American city where he would live and work as an adult.

Just the place for "Ole Hem...to dry out his bones."

Ernest Hemingway first saw Key West in April of 1928. That spring he and his second wife, Pauline Pfeiffer Hemingway, five months pregnant, sailed from Marseilles to Havana. From there they boarded a Peninsular & Occidental steamship bound for the island, just ninety miles away. As the ship crossed the swift, dark Gulf Stream and maneuvered through the Florida Reef, he gazed across clear aqua waters and saw ahead a flat, grayish mass broken only by the town's skyscraper, the seven-story Colonial Hotel, rising like a thick, Key West cigar from a clump of wooden, mostly unpainted buildings. Only as they steamed closer could he begin to make out the island's colors, the brilliant tropical foliage, bougainvillea, hibiscus, oleander, interspersed with green palm fronds.

The heat bothered the Hemingways. Ernest was not dressed for Key West. He was wearing a necktie, hardly part of the town's dress code. Pregnancy made the weather harder for Pauline to take. She wanted her baby born in the United States, but clearly not in a hot, humid, rundown backwater like Key West. The couple planned to stay in Key West only about six weeks and then drive to Piggott, Arkansas, the ancestral home of the Pfeiffers.

Shortly before noon they cleared customs and Ernest began looking for the Model A Ford roadster Pauline's wealthy Uncle Gus had bought for them. Unfortunately, the car had not yet arrived from Miami. Ernest telephoned the Trevor and Morris Company, the local Ford dealership. Apologetic that the car was late, the dealers insisted that the couple take up residence at one of the Trevor and Morris Apartments, upstairs over the garage. A sweat-drenched, irritated Hemingway agreed. He called a taxi to take them and their luggage the four blocks from the P&O docks to their new quarters at 314 Simonton Street.

Florida Photographic Archives

Ernest Hemingway at the typewriter. He actually preferred to write in longhand.

Without the delay the Hemingways' stay in Key West might have been a short one. Fortunately he stayed long enough to realize that the island was right for him. Once he got the necktie off he enjoyed the bone-warming heat. He promptly went to work on a half-finished manuscript, which would become *A Farewell to Arms.* In Paris he had lived and worked in an apartment above a sawmill. Now he found himself trying to complete his novel above a small-town garage. It was, he remarked, a kind of irony he could "damn well do without."

Alvin Morland, a Florida travel writer, visited the island as a boy during the early Hemingway years. He wrote: "We arrived in Key West during the siesta hour when most businesses were closed, but the aroma of strong Cuban coffee permeated the downtown area. The unpainted homes, weathered gray, had balconies. Their sloping roofs were designed to funnel rain water into pipes leading to cisterns, the only source of fresh water in the city. There seemed to be ice cream parlors in every block of the commercial section, and we wasted no time in trying such exotic flavors as coconut, sugar apple and sapodilla. Later we sampled marquitas—fried green plantains sliced as thin as potato chips."

The poet Robert Frost, who visited Key West a few years later, also commented on the roofs in a letter to his fellow-poet Louis Untermeyer: "There is no sanitation. The water is all off the roofs and after it goes through people I don't know where it goes. Everything is shabby and even dilapidated."

Soon after he settled in, Hemingway received a letter forwarded from Paris. The letter informed him that his parents, Dr. Clarence Hemingway, a physician, and his wife, Grace, were in Florida. His father, whose home was in Oak Park, Illinois, was inspecting land he owned in St. Petersburg. Actually Ernest's parents were a good bit closer.

The writer was fishing from the Trumbo pier when he heard a familiar bobwhite whistle. It was a family signal. He looked up and saw his father waving to him from a P&O steamship.

Ernest was saddened to observe his father's deteriorating health. He was, however, glad that his parents got along quite well with

Pauline. The four of them had dinner downtown, probably at Delmonico's at 218 Duval Street. For fifty cents the restaurant featured a representative Cuban/Key West dinner of arroz con pollo, green turtle steak, fish and Spanish garbanzos. After a tour of the island guided by Ernest, the elder Hemingway boarded the 5:40 P.M. train for Miami.

A week after Ernest and Pauline landed at Key West, Uncle Gus's yellow roadster was delivered. Soon Hemingway was driving up the highway some twenty miles to the No Name Key ferryboat docks and fishing from the landing there.

One day George "Georgie" Brooks, prosecuting attorney for Monroe County, was waiting for the ferry boat from Lower Matecumbe Key. He noticed a new face, a big, rugged fisherman, wearing canvas shorts, a fish-stained pullover shirt, a cap and dirty tennis shoes. No doubt about it. The man looked suspicious: scars above his right knee—from an Austrian .420 shell wound in World War I—and a particularly nasty purple scar above his right eye. Could the man with the rod and reel be a lawbreaker on the run? Or another bootlegger?

Striking up a conversation with him, Brooks soon put his suspicions to rest. The man was writing a book, he said, and resting up after a "bloody awful" winter in Paris. Hemingway probably dodged around any questions about the purple scar, the result of an embarrassingly bizarre accident in France. In the wee hours of a cold March morning he had gone to the bathroom in his apartment. He had sleepily reached up for the chain to flush the toilet. Instead he grasped the cord to the skylight. The glass came crashing down on his head. Nine stitches in an emergency room at 3 A.M. had closed the nasty wound.

Hemingway asked Brooks if he knew anyone with a boat who would be willing to share fishing expenses. The attorney told him to go to the Thompson Hardware Store on Caroline Street and introduce himself to Charles Thompson.

"He likes to fish as well as any man I know," said Brooks. "He'll take you out. Just tell him I sent you by."

The lawyer would become one of Hemingway's closest friends,

but not as close as the man he sent him to see. Ernest picked up his rod and reel and the hog snappers he had caught and drove back to Key West.

Clad in khakis, Charles, a member of the island's most affluent family, was standing behind a counter when Hemingway walked in. Their handshake initiated one of the most enduring friendships of the author's life. They made arrangements to go out fishing the next evening.

After he closed the store, Charles walked to his home at 1029 Fleming Street. That night he told his wife, Lorine, about the man he had met.

"Georgie Brooks sent him by. Says his name's Hemingway. Said George told him I liked to fish and might take him out. Says he's written a couple of books."

A couple of books? By April of 1928 the 29-year-old Hemingway already had six published books to his credit, most notably *Men Without Women*, a volume of short stories, and the internationally acclaimed novel, *The Sun Also Rises.*

He was a celebrity in Paris and in much of the United States. But in Key West he was an unknown. And he liked it that way.

CHAPTER II

HEMINGWAY'S MOB

THE DAY AFTER HEMINGWAY MET THOMPSON the two of them boarded Charles's 18-foot powerboat and followed the channel through Key West Bight to the Gulf of Mexico. An evening of fishing brought them several sizable tarpon, a fighting gamefish known as the Silver King. The magic of Key West was beginning to seduce Ernest. Free of distractions, he could concentrate on *A Farewell to Arms* during the mornings, then relax in the afternoons or evenings with a rod and reel.

Soon Thompson invited the Hemingways over to dinner at their home, only a few blocks away from the Trevor and Morris Apartments. Lorine entertained them in true Key West style. She had Phoebe, her black Bahamian cook, prepare a conch dinner for their visitors who had only recently dined in the brasseries of Paris. Phoebe cooked black beans and yellow rice and a Keys delicacy, green turtle steak. One of the many businesses of the wealthy Thompson family was a cannery that processed turtle meat for steaks and soup. To round out the meal Phoebe served them a raw conch meat salad and Cuban bread. Ernest brought a European touch to the occasion with several bottles of a good red Chianti wine.

Hemingway lavishly praised the island cooking. Phoebe was delighted. "That mon Hem'n'way one fine eater," she said.

Ernest also offered impressive proof that he was indeed an author. He gave Charles a copy of *The Sun Also Rises*, inscribed "To Charles Thompson from his friend Ernest Hemingway, Key West

1928," and one of *Men Without Women,* with an even more personal message, "To Charles Thompson with all best wishes—and many tarpon—from his friend Ernest Hemingway, Key West, 1928."

It was a good evening for all concerned. Ernest and Charles had a few Scotches after dinner, then walked along tree-shaded Fleming Street, talking about hunting and fishing. Pregnant Pauline, increasingly uncomfortable in their stuffy apartment, relaxed with Lorine on the Thompson's breezy front porch. As they talked, a bond began to form between them that paralleled the closeness their husbands were building. The two men and the two women would remain fast friends the rest of their lives.

A native of Georgia, Lorine graduated from Agnes Scott College in Decatur, near Atlanta, in 1919. Two years later she came to Key West to teach social science and soon became head of the Social Science Department at Key West High School. She married Charles on September 6, 1923. Pauline, an heiress, had graduated from the University of Missouri. In France she had been a fashion writer for the Paris edition of *Vogue* magazine. The two women found they had much in common. Both had been born into rural communities in the South, both had been well educated and both had moved on out into a bigger world.

Pauline's father, Paul Pfeiffer, president of the Piggott Custom Gin Company, came to Key West to see his new son-in-law. They installed him in the Key West Colonial Hotel, which offered lodging on both the European and American plans from $1 to $6 a day. Pauline, anxious to get away from the heat, wanted the three of them to drive to Piggott. Ernest protested. He finally agreed to let her leave early by train with a promise that he and her father would follow shortly.

Hemingway liked to surround himself with a circle of cronies, a "Mob." He sent out letters inviting a number of old friends to join him in the "St. Tropez of the poor." He wrote to two artist friends, Henry Strater and Waldo Peirce, to Bill Smith, a boyhood friend from Horton Bay, Michigan, and to Dos Passos.

While awaiting their arrival, he added to his Mob a number of locals whose company he enjoyed. With the exception of Charles, most of them were saddled with colorful nicknames. Joe Russell, a Conch who owned two basic generators of income, a charterboat and a speakeasy, was "Josie" or "Sloppy Joe," a name he gave to a legal bar he opened after Prohibition was repealed. Four other charterboat fisherman were Mobsters: Hamilton Adams, "Sack of Ham" or "Sacker"; Captain Eddie Saunders, "Bra"; and his half brother Captain Burge Saunders; and Jakie Key. A local newspaperman, Earl Adams, became "Jewfish." Adams, who became a close friend, was Keys bureau chief for the *Miami Herald.* During his newspaper days he also worked for the *Key West Citizen*, the *Key West Morning Journal* and the *Baltimore International News.* J. B. Sullivan, an Irishman who owned a machine shop, was "Sully." Ernest had his share of nicknames. He was called the "Old Master" and after being observed with a towel wrapped around his head he was also classified as the "Mahatma." Later in Key West he would assume the father-image name he liked best—"Papa."

By the last week in May all the out-of-town talent had arrived, Dos Passos, "Dos"; Henry Strater, "Mike"; Waldo Peirce, "Don Pico"; and Bill Smith, "Old Bill." Bypassing the island's luxury hotel, the Casa Marina, "rooms from $7," Ernest booked them into the one-hundred-room Overseas Hotel, a three-story wood hostelry at 917 Fleming Street. Room rates: a dollar a day. Charles pronounced them "as grand a group of men as ever came together."

Thompson connections gave them access to the clear blue-green waters at the Navy Yard. There the men swam together and cheered and jeered at Hemingway's specialty dive, a combination of bellybuster and swan dive. They called it the "Hemingswan."

For breakfast they liked the bare-bones Electric Kitchen, a one-story wooden building at 830 Fleming Street. The owner and cook was Mrs. Rhoda Baker, better known as Rutabaga. A "club breakfast" at the Electric Kitchen cost 20 to 45 cents; lunch and dinner, 30 to 50 cents.

Some of their dinners were enjoyed at the Thompson's home, where they feasted on the cooking of Phoebe. When they went together as a group for dinner, they usually picked Delmonico's or Ramon's, both on Duval Street.

After one of Phoebe's dinners they often strolled east on Fleming Street to Valladares Book Store, where they browsed through books and magazines. Leonte Valladares, a 30-year-old Cuban, had agreed to stock Hemingway's hardback books. He charged a dollar extra for autographed copies of *The Sun Also Rises* and *Men Without Women.* Through Valladares Hemingway subscribed to the New York papers, the *Times,* the *Herald-Tribune,* the *World-Telegram,* the *Mirror* and the *Daily News.* The papers were delivered by the proprietor's young son, Arthur. He recalled his first meeting with Hemingway:

Florida Photographic Archives

Duval Street in the 1930s when Hemingway's Mob ranged up and down the streets of Key West.

"He came into my father's store, wearing moccasins and a pair of shorts held up with a rope. 'This man is poor, he doesn't have a belt,' I said to my father in Spanish. What I didn't know was that Hemingway understood Spanish. He picked me up and sat me down in his lap and told me in Spanish an Indian legend about how moccasins were made."

A rowdy bunch, the Mob liked to carouse in the evenings. One of their favorites was Raul's Club on East Roosevelt Boulevard, which commanded a view of the Atlantic. A live orchestra played and couples danced on "the finest dance floor in the city." A bizarre feature was a tank of groupers trained by Raul Vasquez himself to perform in their tank as he fed them by hand.

In Old Town they visited Pena's Garden of Roses, a beer garden nestled among rose bushes. Another popular spot was the Tropical Club on the corner of Front and Fitzpatrick streets. Its sign called it the place "where good fellows get together." At 1111 Duval Street they visited the Cuban Cafe, which offered "foreign and domestic beer—anything you want."

To cap off the first assembling of the Mob, Ernest planned a weekend fishing trip to the Dry Tortugas. He hired Captain Bra Saunders and his charterboat along with Bra's brother, Burge, as mate. On a Friday afternoon in the third week in May they set out for the islands west of Key West—Ernest, Dos, Waldo, Mike and the poet, Archibald MacLeish, an old friend from Paris who had joined them in Key West. Charles trailed Captain Bra's charterboat in his 18-footer. Burge rode with him.

Just before dusk they anchored in the Marquesas Islands. They swam in the clear waters near the boat and caught fish for dinner, unaware that underneath the gulf's sandy bottom lay the three-hundred-million dollar-treasure of the *Nuestra Senora de Atocha,* a Spanish galleon wrecked on the reef in 1622. Next morning at dawn they arose for a breakfast of thick Cuban coffee, Cuban bread, avocadoes and smoked fish.

Both boats went out in quest of the Silver King—the giant tarpon for which the Marquesas were famous. The prize went to the rugged, bearded Waldo Peirce who battled a 183½ pound tarpon for two hours before pulling it to shore.

Early the next morning a low-pressure ridge convinced Charles, a man who knew the vagaries of Keys weather, that he had better head his 18-footer back to safe harbor closer to Key West. Captain Bra's charterboat continued its westward cruise toward the Dry Tortugas. Just before dark Captain Bra tied up at the docks at historic Fort Jefferson. Built before the Civil War as a defense outpost and a coaling station, Fort Jefferson later became famous as the prison that housed Dr. Samuel Mudd, the Maryland doctor who set the broken leg of John Wilkes Booth after the assassination of President Abraham Lincoln. Don Pico's fishing skills deserted him in the Tortugas. He hooked, then lost, seven straight tarpon before finally landing one. The following morning they left Fort Jefferson for the ten-hour cruise back to Key West. The weather conditions that sent Thompson back early presented no problems for Captain Bra.

By the end of May all the out-of-town Mobsters had left on the FEC train out of Key West. Ernest figured it was time for him and Paul Pfeiffer to join Pauline in Piggott, Arkansas, a 1400-mile drive. Before leaving he asked Lorine to find a house for him and Pauline for the next season of 1929. She didn't think he was serious about it.

In late May of 1928 leaving Key West by automobile was no easy task. Although the railroad had been in place since 1912, U.S. 1, the Overseas Highway, was missing a few stretches of pavement. They drove to No Name Key, where Ernest had met Georgie Brooks. From there they took the 9 A.M. ferry to Lower Matecumbe Key, a five-hour trip covering some 41 miles. From the town of Islamorada they picked up U.S. 1 and drove across concrete and rickety wooden bridges, finally crossing a long, wooden bridge at Ocean Reef. They arrived at Florida City on the mainland just before sunset.

The next time Hemingway returned to Key West, in the fall of 1928, he would bring with him a new baby. After an 18-hour labor, Pauline had delivered Patrick Hemingway, a nine-and-a-half-pound boy, in Kansas City, Missouri, on June 28, 1928.

CHAPTER III

◆ ◆ ◆ ◆ ◆ ◆ ◆ ◆ ◆ ◆ ◆

THE HOUSE ON WHITEHEAD STREET

FIND US A HOUSE for next winter. That's what the Hemingways asked Lorine Thompson. Then they left for Kansas City, where Pauline would give birth to their first child. Charles Thompson did not expect them to return.

"It was fun but we've seen the last of that gang," he said sadly.

Charles was wrong. They came back in November, 1928 and again in February of 1930. Ernest told Charles he would like to look around Key West for "a place to hang my hat." Nothing came of it, probably because he and Charles were more skilled in hunting down sailfish than houses.

What they didn't know was that Lorine had already shown Pauline a big, two-story, rundown stone house at 907 Whitehead Street, set on a scrubbily landscaped acre and a half. "A miserable wreck of a house," Lorine called it. To Pauline it was "a damned haunted house."

When the Hemingways returned in the spring of 1931, they realized the time had come to settle down in Key West. Pauline's Uncle Gus Pfeiffer, who had already given them a Ford for a wedding present, told his favorite niece he would buy a house for them whenever they were ready.

By now Ernest and Pauline knew what they wanted. Ernest

needed a secluded place to write. Pauline wanted a setting with a European flavor. And both agreed they needed plenty of living space. By this time Pauline was pregnant again so they would be requiring a yard where two children could play.

"Well, there's always the haunted house," said Lorine.

They took a second look. This time Pauline saw something different—not the neglect of the past but rather the potential of the future. The old Spanish colonial mansion, built in 1851 by the shipping magnate Asa Tift, was actually a magnificent structure, well-suited for the subtropical world of the island. Uncle Gus sold a few shares in Hudnut and let Sloan's Liniment pay for the house for Ernest and Pauline. It was purchased for $8000 on April 29, 1931 from Florida First National Bank, the same bank that had refused to cash a royalty check for him three years earlier. Three thousand dollars of the purchase price went to pay off back taxes. Times were hard in Key West in 1931.

"Uncle Gus was a small, nostalgic man, the big wheel in Hudnut's in New York," wrote John Dos Passos. "Stiff with money and having neither chick nor child as the saying was, he lavished attention on his smart pretty nieces. Ernest fascinated him. Hunting, fishing, writing. He wanted to help Ernest do all the things he'd been too busy making money to do."

The day after the sale a story in the *Key West Citizen* reported: "Mr. and Mrs. Hemingway have spent a number of winters in Key West. They like the climate here so well and enjoy fishing so much that they decided to invest in a residence.

"The place they have acquired is conceded to be one of the most ideally located homesites in the city. With but little improvement of the large lawn and substantial building, the premises will become one of the most beautiful spots in Key West." Ernest also told the paper a $500 contract had already been let to start work on the house immediately.

That night Ernest and Charles celebrated by getting drunk at Josie Russell's speakeasy. The Thompsons were, of course, delighted that their new friends would be settling into Key West permanently. The next day they were dismayed by Pauline's announcement that work on the house would have to wait till next winter. Within a week the Hemingways, Ernest, Pauline and young Patrick, going on three, were on their way to Spain. There Ernest would continue work on a book he was writing on bullfighting. The sport, or art, as some would call it, had enthralled him since he ran with the bulls at Pamplona, then wrote about the happening in *The Sun Also Rises*.

The Hemingways did not move in until just before Christmas. It was a difficult time for Pauline. Her second child, Gregory, had been born on November 12, 1931, again in Kansas City by Caesarian section. She was still weak when they arrived in Key West.

The main body of the house they moved into in December was constructed of white coral rock, cut from the property to create a giant hole which became one of the few basements in south Florida. Heart of white pine had been shipped to Key West from Asa Tift's lands in Tifton, Georgia, a town he had helped found. Built in Spanish colonial style, the Tift home had for years been an island showplace. Such was not the case when Uncle Gus forked over his $8000.

Florida Photographic Archives

The house on Whitehead Street, in need of landscaping.

Putting the house into livable condition helped solve some of Key West's dreadful unemployment problems. The house swarmed with out-of-work Conchs, noisily and happily putting the place back in order. The crew turned first to a two-story outbuilding, a carriage house in the rear of the house. The second floor of this building would become the studio where Ernest could write. An iron catwalk was built from his second-story bedroom across to his workroom. He was usually at his writing table by 8 A.M., starting each day with a battery of sharpened pencils. "A seven pencil morning" was a productive day's work for him.

Cabinet-maker Toby Bruce came all the way from Piggott, Arkansas, to build bookcases for the studio, the first of many construction projects he would perform for Hemingway. Plaster cracks were repaired and the room was repainted a light sea-green. Toby located an old gateleg table, which became the author's desk, and a wooden cigarmaker's chair with a wide leather bottom and a narrow leather backpiece.

While the work went on, Hemingway struggled to shut out the noise as he continued writing *Death in the Afternoon.* His studio was soon littered with notes on bullfighting and photographs he would use in the book. Pauline told Lorine his study looked like "a lightly organized waste paper can."

By April of 1932 Hemingway was delighted with the progress on the house. He wrote his old friend, the painter Waldo Peirce: "This is a grand house. Do you remember it across from the lighthouse. One that looked like a pretty good Utrillo, somwhere between that and Miró's Farm."

From Hemingway, this was high praise. Joan Miró's painting, "The Farm," displaying a Spanish farmhouse and farmyard, was one of his favorites. He had bought it for his first wife, Hadley, as a birthday present, then had borrowed it after their divorce and never returned it.

Still recovering from the ordeal of Gregory's Caesarian birth, Pauline spent much of her time in bed. For their first Christmas in their first home, a tree was erected at the foot of her bed.

By midwinter the house on Whitehead Street was becoming a home. The structure had been rewired, the plumbing repaired, ceilings and walls replastered, new wooden floors installed and the leaky roof fixed. The basement, fourteen feet deep, had been converted into a wine cellar for Ernest's European wines.

During their trips to the continent the Hemingways had acquired many Spanish antiques. These were shipped to Key West, along with several chandeliers of hand-blown Venetian glass. Eighteenth-century Spanish furniture in the dining room included a dining table, a sideboard and chairs designed to provide guests with a close and convenient place to hang their swords. At Hemingway's guests would have been more likely to bring boxing gloves.

Most of the interior furnishings bore Pauline's stamp. Ernest's biggest contribution to the house's decor during the Key West years came from hunting trophies. Impressive heads of various big game animals he had killed in the Rockies and in Africa showed up around the house. A mounted wildebeest, hardly a thing of beauty, hung on the dining room wall. Pauline supervised the landscaping of the property, including the planting of a banyan tree on the south side of the house.

Meanwhile Toby Bruce was kept busy building emperor tables, wine racks and an emporer-sized bed. His work on the house would go on for years. Later he would build a brick wall around the property partly to discourage nosy sightseers, and partly to keep the active Hemingway boys inside.

In 1937 Toby oversaw the construction of the Keys' first swimming pool. Pauline, sensing she was losing Ernest, decided to surprise him with a grand gesture. Since he loved to swim, why not his own private pool in the spacious backyard? It could be ready for him when he returned from his lengthy tour of duty covering the Spanish Civil War.

The hunter home from the hills was not pleased. When he learned that the pool cost $20,000, two-and-a-half times the purchase price of the house, he took a penny out of his pocket and flung it to the ground. You might as well take my last cent, he told her. Retrieving the penny, she had it preserved in cement and covered with glass, much to the delight many decades later of the sightseers Hemingway had hoped to keep at bay.

Saving the penny added a light touch to an absurd scene, but the incident only pointed up one of the reasons their marriage would eventually fall apart. The money Pauline spent on the pool was hers, not his. Pfeiffer money supported Ernest in style for years. A proud, macho man, he could only have been resentful.

The famous urinal from Sloppy Joe's. *Photo by Stuart McIver*

In the lushly landscaped gardens near the pool a urinal from Sloppy Joe's has been laid out on the ground to serve as a watering trough for the Hemingway cats. Dressed up with tile and a Spanish olive jar, it adds an attractive touch to the scene. And for the tour guides it always brings a snicker from the tourists who have made the Hemingway House and Museum the island's most popular attraction.

CHAPTER IV

◆ ◆ ◆ ◆ ◆ ◆ ◆ ◆ ◆ ◆ ◆

THE SPORTING LIFE

HEMINGWAY WAS A SPORTS FAN. He wrote about fishing in the Nick Adams stories, about hunting in *Green Hills of Africa*, about bullfighting in *Death in the Afternoon*, about baseball and football broadcasting in "The Gambler, the Nun and the Radio," about horse racing in "My Old Man" and about prize-fighting in "Fifty Grand." He hunted in Wyoming, France and Kenya, fished the freshwater rivers of Michigan and the West and the salt waters of the Gulf Stream and the Caribbean and boxed wherever he could find a ring and a willing sparring partner. As a spectator, he loved the bullfights in Spain, heavyweight championship boxing matches in New York and cockfighting in Key West.

Hunting was out of the question in his new hometown since houses and buildings occupied most of the island. But fishing in Florida Bay, the Gulf of Mexico and the Gulf Stream was superb. And luckily for Ernest, fight night arrived every other Friday.

At the poorly lighted Key West Arena on the northeast corner of Thomas and Petronia streets, island boxers, mostly blacks, mixed it up before cheering Conchs, who were looking for inexpensive entertainment in the hard times of the Depression. Ringside seats cost $3, general admission to the grandstand, $1.25. The fights usually drew several hundred spectators. Fighters paid from the gate picked up $25-30 a fight.

James "Iron Baby" Roberts, a light heavyweight, was still in his teens when he first saw the celebrated author at the Key West Arena.

"Hemingway looked like an ordinary hippie," Iron Baby told Paul Heidelberg, who wrote about the Key West fight scene in *Sports Illustrated* in December of 1985. "I always tell people that it was the first time I saw a hippie, because he used to dress that way. He had a long beard, and he needed a haircut, and he was wearing shorts and an old shirt, just like a common person. You'd never have guessed that he was the big writer he was. He carried right on like everyday people. That's the way he lived here."

That night Hemingway was refereeing the main event, a bout between Alfred "Black Pie" Colebrooks and a talented Cuban fighter with an Anglicized name, Joe Mills. Working in Colebrooks' corner was Kermit "Battling Geech" Forbes, better known as "Shine."

Mills kept belting Black Pie to the canvas, "about eight times," Forbes recalls. Black Pie was game, maybe too game. He kept getting up.

"This is enough," said Forbes. He threw in the towel, a signal that Colebrooks' corner wanted the fight awarded to Mills on a technical knockout.

Hemingway threw the towel back. Forbes threw it back in and back out it came. After the third unsuccessful towel-tossing Shine Forbes jumped into the ring and swung at Hemingway, a futile venture since the author towered more than half a foot above the enraged Forbes. The furious fighter couldn't reach him. He tried jumping up but after he swung he fell against Hemingway's chest. The author grabbed him by both ears and shook him. Policeman arrived to arrest Forbes.

"No, don't arrest him," said Hemingway. "Anytime a man's got guts enough to take a punch at me, he's all right."

"I didn't know who he was," Forbes said. "Nobody told me. I thought he was some bum trying to pick up a dollar. When I got home my mother said, 'Do you realize who you just took a punch at? It was Mr. Ernest Hemingway, the famous writer.' I went over to Hemingway's house that night to apologize. Hemingway shook my hand and then challenged me to come over the next day. That's when our sparring began."

Hemingway Days Festival

"Iron Baby" Roberts, left, and "Shine" Forbes recapture their glory days as boxers in the 1930s.

Hemingway set up a boxing ring near the swimming pool in his backyard. He had two speed punching bags and one heavy bag and three kinds of gloves—eight, ten and sixteen ounces. At one time or another all the local fighters sparred with him at fifty cents a round. All, the story goes, were beaten by him, but, said Iron Baby some years later, "We all took it easy on Mr. Ernest. We'd go about three or four rounds with him. I was the only one he was kind of leery of, on account of my weight. We were pretty young then, and Hemingway was older than us, but he'd give us a tussle. I didn't wear any headgear, but Hemingway did. Geech didn't wear any headgear, either."

In World War II Roberts would become a ranking light heavyweight and Forbes a ranking lightweight in the Army. Black Pie, just 15 at the time of his losing battle with Mills, later studied music at the Bradley University Conservatory of Music. Iron Baby Roberts later spoke highly of the treatment of blacks by Hemingway and the people of Key West.

"The average person in Key West didn't believe in this segregated stuff with black and white. We all lived next door to each other. We didn't know anything about white sections and black sections. I was raised with white guys; Hemingway was friendly with black people. But the whole town was that way."

One Christmas Hemingway threw a big outdoor party at his Whitehead Street house. Part of the entertainment was a boxing exhibition put on by Roberts, Forbes and other Key West pugilists. Among the celebrity guests that night was Gene Tunney, former world's heavyweight champion, the boxer who dethroned the great Jack Dempsey. The fighters were paid after the hat was passed. Tunney, the only one of the guests who talked to the fighters, deposited $200 in the hat.

Hemingway's most famous Key West fight occurred outside the ring. In 1929 Ernest's sister, Madelaine, better known as Sunny, had just finished typing her brother's manuscript for *A Farewell to Arms.* To celebrate she relaxed later that day at a cocktail party at a home on Flagler Street, near the South Street house the Hemingways had been renting. During the party the famous American poet Wallace Stevens, who was also an insurance company executive in Hartford, Connecticut, belittled her brother's writing. Sunny left the party, close to tears. When she told Ernest what had happened, he headed straight for the party, called Stevens outside and broke his jaw with one punch. While his sterling defense of his sister was commendable, Hemingway was somewhat remorseful. Stevens was a good twenty years older and quite portly.

Later Stevens apologized for his rudeness to Sunny but refused to back down on his low opinion of Hemingway's writing. In the 1950s each of them would win Pulitzer Prizes, Stevens for poetry, Hemingway for his novel, *The Old Man and the Sea.*

Cock fights were held on a large, open lot in the southwestern section of the city, just off Amelia Street near the black district. In the center of the lot a circular area was fenced in to form an arena for the roosters. Bleachers on the north and south sides of the arena provided seats for about a hundred spectators.

Following the Latin tradition of the bullfight, trainers and handlers began to arrive with their fighting cocks, carried in brightly colored cages. Soon a noisy crowd assembled. Cubans and Conchs gathered around the arena, wearing their Sunday best: white suits, loud ties and Panama hats. Vendors were on hand, selling homemade frozen popsicles and hot tacos. Homemade wine and Hoover Gold, the Conchs' derisive name for bootleg whiskey, were passed around.

Just before 1 P.M. the big bettors showed up. The wealthiest of the Cubans, usually the bolita bankers, who ran the island's numbers racket, the most affluent of the Conchs and the town's political leaders parked on Emma Street and strutted down Amelia Street to the scene of the action. Promptly at one handlers faced off following the traditional challenge.

"You want to fight your rooster?"

"Yes, I want to fight my rooster."

The gamebirds were bred and trained to kill. Some sported razor-sharp artificial talons. The length of the match was limited by an hourglass set for fifteen or thirty minutes—or by the death of one of the fighters.

Betting between fans began immediately. Tens of thousands of dollars could change hands on a given Sunday, and none but an expert would be aware of anything happening except in the arena. Victory came when a rooster was so weakened by pecks or slashes from spurs that he was unable to continue. Usually the fighting cocks died. If not, they were killed. A draw, which meant that no money changed hands, was considered such a disgrace that the shamed roosters had their necks wrung. After the fights, bettors adjourned to motel or hotel rooms or to speakeasies to settle their bets. A winner could pocket as much as $10,000 on a winning Sunday.

Hemingway enjoyed the color and excitement of the sport, conducted within easy walking distance of his home. Cockfighting was, of course, illegal.

Despite his love of the sporting life, Hemingway was not always a sporting man. His closest friend, Charles Thompson, was horrified when Ernest shot an eagle on a hunting trip in the Rockies. Poet Archibald MacLeish likewise was disturbed when the novelist shot terns for target practice and let their bodies just drop into the sea.

In the summer of 1915 when he was sixteen, Ernest was involved in an illegal shooting incident at Walloon Lake in Michigan. He and his sister Sunny were exploring the lake area. Ernest flushed a blue heron out of the reeds, then shot it. He knew the act was against the law, but he figured the large wading bird would make a handsome addition to his father's collection of stuffed birds.

Unfortunately for young Ernest, game wardens learned that he had killed a protected bird. When they arrived at the Hemingway house, the boy had already fled the area on the advice of his mother. Later that summer his father advised him to come out of hiding and face up to what he had done. He pleaded guilty before a judge and paid a fine of $15.

Years later in Key West Ernest often engaged the services of a commercial fisherman and skilled boatman named Morrell Bradley, who worked with him aboard *Pilar*. Hemingway knew that Morrell was the oldest son of Guy Morrell Bradley, the first Audubon warden killed in the line of duty while working near Oyster Keys in Florida Bay. Guy's principal job was protecting the large wading birds of South Florida, among them the Florida members of the species Hemingway had shot in Michigan.

CHAPTER V

❖ ❖ ❖ ❖ ❖ ❖ ❖ ❖ ❖ ❖ ❖

PILAR

NOT SINCE HIS BOYHOOD DAYS on Lake Walloon, in northern Michigan, in the land of his Nick Adams stories, had Hemingway had a boat of his own. The time had come for him to move past chartering boats or fishing from one of his friend's boats. The Old Master craved mightily a sports fishing boat owned outright by himself, named by him and built to his specifications. He had learned enough about the seas around Key West, about the Gulf Stream, to know exactly what he wanted. In the catalogue of the Wheeler Shipyard in Brooklyn he had found his dreamboat—a diesel-powered 38-footer with twin screws, double rudders, ample bunk space and the kind of seaworthiness that could stand up to the action of the Gulf Stream. The price for the 38-footer was $7500, a lot of money in 1934, but his fortunes were clearly improving.

After his African safari in the spring of 1934, Hemingway boarded the *Ile de France* to return to New York. There he made two important visits. The first was to *Esquire*, a new men's magazine for which he was already writing. Always a persuasive man, he talked editor Arnold Gingrich into advancing him a hefty $3300 against future magazine stories. Next, armed with his *Esquire* check, he piled into a cab with Pauline and headed for Brooklyn, to the Wheeler Shipyard. He used the check as a down payment on the boat of his dreams. She would have Wheeler's standard 38-foot hull, planked with white cedar and framed with steam-bent white oak. The forward cabin would be a double stateroom. In addition, the boat would have a head, two bunks and a dinette, complete with galley and ice box.

Hemingway added a few touches of his own. He had the stern cut down a foot to reduce the distance a fish had to be lifted to bring it aboard. He planned on reeling in trophy catches. And to make it easier to pull large fish into the cockpit he had a large wooden roller installed over the transom. Delivery was promised in thirty days, F.O.B. Miami.

He had already picked out the name for his boat. It proved to be one that overjoyed Pauline. One of her little-used nicknames was *Pilar.* And *Pilar* became the name of one of the world's most famous sports fishing cruisers. Pauline had to share the honor of the name with a Catholic bullfight shrine in Zaragosa, Spain.

Back in Key West Ernest started to work on the safari book he would call *Green Hills of Africa.* The evening of May 9, 1934, he and Pauline were entertaining a convivial group of guests that included John and Katy Dos Passos, the Thompsons and Hemingway's nineteen-year-old brother, Leicester, nicknamed "the Baron" by Ernest but generally called Les. Word came that *Pilar* had just arrived by rail in Miami. The party turned even more festive. The next day Hemingway dropped work on his book. He and Captain Bra Saunders took the afternoon train to Miami to pick up the cruiser. Hemingway and Bra launched *Pilar* into Biscayne Bay and headed south through the Keys. As Ernest stood behind the wheel, he gazed down on a bronze plaque that read:

HULL 576
Wheeler Shipyard
Boat Manufactuers
1934
Brooklyn, New York

On its maiden voyage a representative from Wheeler traveled with them, checking out the engines, a 75- horsepower Chrysler with a reduction gear to turn a powerful, slow-speed propeller and a 40-horsepower Lycoming for trolling. The boat could do a full sixteen knots on a calm sea.

Captain Hemingway steered *Pilar*, freshly varnished and gleaming with its coat of black paint, into the Key West Navy Yard. He had already obtained permission from the commanding officer to dock his boat there free of charge. The Mob was waiting on the submarine docks. When *Pilar* cruised into the basin, the Mobsters let out a big whoop and blew horns to celebrate the event.

Captain Hemingway checks out *Pilar*. *Monroe County Library*

That night glasses were raised to toast the boat Ernest called "the new skiff." Bra was warm in praise of *Pilar*. "Now you boys know somethin' about boats.... This one rides so high, lighter than any craft around here, or the Bahama boats or the Cubans either. She whines like her big engine is burnin' up, but it's not. It's the reduction gear."

In his book *My Brother, Ernest Hemingway*, the Baron gave an eye-witness account of *Pilar's* shakedown cruise. Pauline had brought hampers of sandwiches, fruit, beer, cold drinks, and ice as well as paper towels and napkins to keep the scene neat. Ernest trolled the eastern dry rocks, the Sand Key area, the western dry rocks, then back again. They encountered no large billfish but caught a few barracuda and grouper and one amberjack.

The skipper didn't seem to mind. Hemingway was using the first cruise to get the feel of the boat. At a speed of ten knots he swung *Pilar* into a hard turn to starboard and then to port. Then he opened both engines up and *Pilar,* wrote Leicester, "seemed to plane," throwing back a great wake. Ernest brought his craft up to better than fifteen knots.

Hemingway turned the wheel over to his younger brother and moved around the boat, checking for vibration, feeling the temperatures, testing the engine hatches. "I want to know what she's like all over," he said and he wandered all over the boat to get the feel and the sound of *Pilar* running through the water.

The knowledge he gained from the performance of the boat in a wide variety of conditions, the Baron concluded, "proved invaluable in handling the *Pilar* in foul weather."

Near the end of May Ernest finally boated the kind of fish he had envisioned for *Pilar,* the biggest Atlantic sailfish ever taken on rod and reel. Unfortunately it could not be claimed as an official world's record.

A visiting Catholic priest from Miami had been invited to fish with Ernest and Leicester. They had cruised out to the Gulf Stream near the Marquesas. By 3:30 that afternoon they had had little success, but Hemingway was relaxed, well plied with sandwiches and beer.

"Sun and sea air, as they dry your body, make for almost effortless beer consumption," he said. "The body needs liquid of a nourishing kind. The palate craves coolness. The optic nerve delights in the sensation of chill that comes from its nearness to the palate as you swallow. Then the skin suddenly blossoms with thousands of happy beads of perspiration as you quaff."

Suddenly, a cry from Father McGrath broke through the lyrical tribute to beer. The priest had hooked himself a billfish.

"Reel as fast as you can, Father," said Ernest, but a shark seized the fish. Soon the priest had hooked another, this one a monster of a sailfish.

"Fight him, Father," called the skipper, maneuvering his *Pilar* skillfully.

Twenty-eight times the fish jumped. Father McGrath, hampered by arthritis in his left hand, tired after some fifteen minutes of trying to hold the mighty leaper.

"Ernest, you must help me. I can't handle this fish any longer."

"Look, he's yours," said Hemingway. "He's a sailfish, not a marlin as I first thought. He may be of record size. If I take over, the fish will be disqualified for any kind of record."

"But I can't go on."

Leicester took the wheel from his brother and Ernest relieved a weary Father McGrath. He battled the fish for nearly three-quarters of an hour. Finally he pulled the fish aboard. It measured over nine feet in length and weighed 119½ pounds. For the rest of his life Hemingway could legitimately claim he had boated the largest Atlantic sailfish ever taken on rod and reel—but he couldn't claim it as an official record. Hemingway docked at Charles Thompson's docks at the foot of Caroline Street. There they strung the giant sailfish up and Hemingway proudly posed for a photograph beside the trophy he—and Father McGrath—had reeled in.

"Toast to the good Father," said Ernest, raising a glass back at the house. It was a gracious gesture, since the handling of the rig by two anglers deprived *Pilar* of a major record in her first month of fishing.

After Father McGrath returned to Miami, he typed out a story about the feat and delivered it, along with the photo of Ernest and the fish, to the *Miami Herald.* One morning while working on his African book, Ernest heard a commotion downstairs. He joined Pauline and Leicester, who showed him the *Herald.* The story ran on page one. It was signed "Eye Witness."

"Now who?" mused Ernest. "Of all the.... I wanted him to take credit for the catch."

The fish, mounted by Al Pflueger's taxidermy firm, hung in the lobby of the Miami Rod and Reed Club, crediting Hemingway with catching the largest Atlantic sailfish ever taken.

"It's their lie, not mine," he told Charles. "Let 'em hang it in their joint."

That year Hemingway enrolled *Pilar* in the Biscayne Bay Yacht Club, based in Coconut Grove, Miami. It was registered as a 39-foot cabin cruiser with an 11-foot beam and a three-foot, two-inch draft. Nominated by Norberg Thompson, Charles's older brother, Hemingway had joined the venerable yacht club the previous year. Its members included such eminent boaters as L.H. Baekland, the founder of the plastics industry; Alfred I. DuPont; G.A. Rentschler, founder of Pratt & Whitney Aircraft; Nathanael Herreshoff, one of America's most respected yacht designers; and Arthur Curtis James, reported to be the second richest man in the world. Three of the yachts enrolled at the BBYC exceeded a hundred feet in length. Norberg's boat was the cruiser *Mareta*, 68 feet long.

Other members included the author Charles Baker, a novelist who wrote regularly for *Esquire*, and Grant Mason, Hemingway's friend from Havana, his base for running Pan American Airways' Caribbean operations. Mason, whom Hemingway once described as a "wealthy twerp," was one of the airline's founders. The Mason Hemingway was really friendly with, very friendly in fact, was Grant's wife, the gorgeous Jane.

Why Hemingway joined the Biscayne Bay Yacht Club has never been clear. His son Patrick later recalled: "There were no clubs in Key West. I remember how delighted he was when he joined the club in Miami." Still, Miami attorney Thomas Johnston, the club's treasurer during the 1930s, doesn't recall ever seeing him at the club. Hemingway let his membership lapse after he moved to Cuba at the end of the decade.

For the rest of the spring Hemingway worked steadily on his safari book, limiting his *Pilar* forays to short cruises in the Key West area. Meanwhile, he began to make plans for his first long trip out into the Gulf Stream. His goal was to spend his thirty-fifth birthday, July 21, 1934, aboard *Pilar*, en route to Cuba. His problem lay in assembling a crew capable of heavy-duty sail fishing. For this he needed an experienced captain at the wheel and a mate versed in the difficult task of gaffing large saltwater fish. Hemingway himself had become skillful in handling the wheel, but he wanted more time for fishing.

For mate he sought out Carlos Gutierrez, captain of a Cuban fishing smack. He had known Gutierrez since 1929 when he met him on a fishing trip to the Dry Tortugas. The 55-year-old Cuban agreed, but that failed to solve the need for a captain. Ernest wanted Joe Russell, but Josie turned him down, a sign of changing times. Josie in recent years had made his living by following two illegal occupations—rumrunner and speakeasy operator. With the repeal of Prohibition in 1933 Josie went straight. Rumrunning was no longer necessary and the speakeasy had given way to the saloon. Russell's Sloppy Joe's (now Captain Tony's) at 428 Greene Street, three times the size of his tiny Front Street speakeasy, was consuming all his time. Key West was officially bankrupt but still the Conchs imbibed. Ernest was puzzled at the turndown.

"Times might be hard, Cap," Josie told him, "but ol' Mr. Hoover done put a helluva thirst on all the honest folks."

Hemingway, in baseball cap, aboard *Pilar*. *Sloppy Joe's*

Instead of Sloppy Joe, Hemingway was forced to round out his crew with Charles Lund, a mate on the Key West-Havana ferry, plus two distinguished members from the Academy of Natural Sciences in Philadelphia, Charles M.B. Cadwalader, the director, and Dr. Henry Fowler, chief ichthyologist. He had been corresponding with the academy on research projects involving the marlin.

Off Morro Castle in Havana Harbor *Pilar's* larger engine developed trouble. Hemingway anchored offshore while Lund tried to repair the engine. Morro Castle guards, assuming they were gunrunners, sent an armed patrol boat to investigate. As they prepared to board *Pilar*, Carlos shouted to them the magic words, "El Hemingway! El Hemingway."

The author was already well known and well liked in Havana. The patrol boat captain apologized and retreated. *Pilar* made it to shore on her trolling engine.

Hemingway's first long voyage lasted six weeks. During the outing he continued to work on *Green Hills*, completing more than a hundred pages before returning to Key West. After he completed his manuscript, *Scribner's* magazine paid him $5,000 for the serialization rights to the story of big game hunting in Africa.

A bloody revolt in Cuba ruled out a fishing trip to Havana in the spring of 1935. Instead Hemingway aboard *Pilar* set out for Bimini in the Bahamas, along with John and Katy Dos Passos and the artist Mike Strater. His crew consisted of a couple of experienced Conchs, Bread Pinder and Hamilton "Old Sack of Ham" Adams. They headed for the Gulf Stream, which flows past Bimini, some 230 nautical miles northeast of Key West. The trip would be long enough for Ernest to commit one of the most bizarre blunders of his accident-prone life.

A few hours after his departure Hemingway returned, his legs covered with blood. Leicester drove him to the Key West Marine Hospital. There the strange sequence of events came out.

Hemingway had hooked a shark a short distance out from Key West. He pulled the big beast aboard and prepared to shoot it with his Colt Woodsman .22- caliber pistol. Just as Hemingway fired, the shark jerked suddenly. The shot missed, hitting instead a strip of metal. The bullet broke into small bits, ricocheting into the calves of both Ernest's legs.

Ernest had to stay in bed for three days, while doctors watched for infection. It didn't develop. He felt he got off easy and even managed to laugh at himself. In addition, he delivered to *Esquire* one of the stories he owed the magazine, "On Being Shot," a humorous piece about a fisherman who managed to shoot himself in both legs with one bullet.

Later that spring Hemingway finally made it to Bimini's glorious fishing grounds. Here he and *Pilar* at last began to achieve sportfishing celebrity. Ernest looked forward to stalking the giant bluefin tuna that migrate through Bahamanian seas. One of the problems in fishing for tuna was the attraction the big fish held for Bimini's plentiful sharks. By the time a hefty tuna could be hauled aboard, much of it would already have been eaten by sharks. A tuna in this condition was said to have been "apple cored."

Hemingway developed a new, aggressive style of tuna fishing. Instead of tiring the fish out first, he worked furiously to bring the fish in while it was still quick and strong enough to evade the sharks. The results were spectacular. He caught the first big unmutilated tuna in Bimini. That spring he brought in two huge tuna, one weighing 610 pounds, another 514. His style of fishing became known as "Hemingwaying."

One evening, late in May, Ernest returned from an unsuccessful fishing trip in which the sharks had won. It was dark by the time he docked and washed down the boat. Then a voice came to him from out of the darkness: "Say, aren't you the guy who claims he catches all the fish?"

A large man he didn't know kept goading him. "I figured him

for a mouthy drunk," Ernest later told Leicester.

The goading, including a reference to Hemingway as a "big fat slob," continued until it erupted into a bare-knuckle fight on the docks. Ernest clipped him with several good punches that barely phased him.

"Then I backed off and really got the weight of a pivot swing into the old Sunday punch," said Hemingway. "He landed, and his ass and head hit the planking at the same time."

A crowd of some sixty people gathered to watch the one-sided battle. As the man lay unconscious on the dock, the crew from his boat, *Storm King*, carried him aboard, then rushed him to Miami for medical treatment.

At dinner that night Ernest was worried that he might have injured the man seriously. He was even more worried when he found out who the man was. He turned out to be Joseph Knapp, owner and publisher of *Collier's*, *Woman's Home Companion*, *The American Magazine* and several other publications.

"That's what you call limiting your magazine markets," he said.

The fight, more than his fishing triumphs, catapulted him into legend. Nattie Saunders and a calypso band wrote a song about the fight called "Big Fat Slob." The Compleat Angler, an inn where Ernest stayed while in Bimini, now includes a Hemingway Museum.

In many ways the Bimini trip was a memorable one. Ernest caught a number of large marlin from *Pilar*. He also met Marjorie Kinnan Rawlings, the Florida author who three years later would win a Pulitzer Prize for her memorable novel, *The Yearling*. Both authors shared the same editor, Maxwell Perkins, at Scribner's.

On Bimini Hemingway also got to know another ardent big game fisherman, Michael Lerner, a man whose wealth came from a large chain of women's clothing stores. From their friendship came the International Game Fish Association, which they created to establish standards and rules and determine world's records for fishing. The IGFA is headquartered now in Pompano Beach, Florida.

"At one time Hemingway apparently held at least one Atlantic sailfish record, not well documented," said Michael Leech, president of IGFA. "He's in the same position as Zane Grey. Their catches would have been back in the days before lines were tested, so they're not really official IGFA records."

In 1936 the poet Archibald MacLeish had come down to Key West to visit Hemingway. One hot day the two of them went fishing aboard *Pilar* but the fish weren't biting and soon the talk became as overheated as the summer air. Ernest grew even angrier when MacLeish told him to "have just another drink and calm down." When they decided to continue the discussion on dry land, Ernest eased the boat into the shallows near a small key between Boca Grande and Snipe Keys. Archie went ashore first. Then Ernest backed out of the shoal waters and gunned *Pilar* for Key West.

When he reached home, Pauline wondered why an angry Ernest was muttering to himself. Finally she learned he had marooned his old friend on an island that belonged to Lower Keys mosquitoes.

" You can't do this, Ernest," she said. "You've got to go back and get him. That's all there is to it. He may be going crazy with the insects, and there's no fresh water on any of these keys."

Pauline insisted that Hemingway go back and rescue Archie. He finally gave in, but relations were never again the same for the two acclaimed writers. Leicester included the anecdote in his book about his brother, but MacLeish later said it never happened.

On his return to Havana in the spring of 1936 Hemingway renewed his ties with Gregorio Fuentes, a native of the Canary Islands who captained his own small Cuban fishing smack. They had met in 1928 when Ernest was fishing in the Dry Tortugas. Ten years later Fuentes became the skipper for *Pilar* for $250 a month, enough for the Canary Islander to buy a home in Cojimar, Cuba. He would continue as the boat's skipper on through World War II, when Ernest used it to track German submarines with a group of other patriotic foes of the Nazis, a group he labeled the "Crook Factory." After Hemingway's death, the author's will gave *Pilar* to Gregorio. Later the Castro government seized the famed fishing boat and let her deteriorate. Hopefully someday she can be restored and become part of the country's Hemingway Museum.

Perhaps the finest tribute to fabled *Pilar* is contained in a piece Hemingway wrote for *Holiday* magazine, July, 1949: "She is a really sturdy boat, sweet in any kind of sea."

CHAPTER VI

❖ ❖ ❖ ❖ ❖ ❖ ❖ ❖ ❖ ❖ ❖

THREE FRIENDS ...AND A FOE

ERNEST HEMINGWAY WAS A GREGARIOUS MAN. Making friends came easy for him. Keeping them was another matter. If his friends were fellow writers, he eventually saw them as competitors and all too often turned against them. Key West friendships, by their nature noncompetitive, had staying power.

Three Key Westers were particularly close to him, Charles Thompson and Josie Russell, both Conchs, and Toby Bruce, a transplanted Arkansan. A man as opinionated as Hemingway also needed enemies. In Julius Stone he found a worthy foeman. For a time, Stone was the most powerful man on the island. He was the Kingfish.

THE MIGHTY HUNTER

They could not have been more different: one a tough, intense writer, a bully and a complex intellectual, the other an uncomplicated small-town shopkeeper, a sweet man with a smile for everyone.

Ernest Hemingway, at times a caricature of macho man, had to be first in everything he did: hunting, fishing, boxing, writing. All too often his fierce competitiveness turned him against writer friends he saw as rivals—Gertrude Stein, Sherwood Anderson, John Dos Passos and Scott Fitzgerald.

Charles Thompson, laid-back, easygoing, noncompetitive, fished and hunted just for the fun of it. Free of any needless pressure to prove himself, he just relaxed and outdid Ernest so often it became a source of embarrassment to the Key Wester.

Hemingway, never noted for his sportsmanship, took from Charles what he never took from anyone else. He just forced a rueful grin. He even dedicated a book on hunting in Africa to his Key West friend and neighbor.

The two met on Hemingway's first day in Key West in April, 1928. An avid freshwater fisherman, Ernest began looking for an equally dedicated saltwater fisherman with a boat. He was referred to Thompson, clearly a man with a boat. In fact, the mighty Thompson family, among its many enterprises, owned a fleet of some 125 fishing boats.

Charles's grandfather was a Norwegian, who was shipwrecked in the Keys, liked the place and stayed on to found what would become the largest business empire on the island. He Americanized the family name from Norberg to Thompson.

By the time Hemingway arrived in Key West, the Thompsons reigned as the town's most affluent family. At one time or another they owned and operated Thompson's Docks (now the Land's End Marina); a fleet of fishing boats; a fish processing company; a marine hardware and tackle shop, run by Charles; an icehouse; a cigarbox factory; a trucking company; a pineapple plantation; a guava jelly factory; and a turtle fishing business which included a fleet of turtle boats, the

Photo by Stuart McIver

The Turtle Kraals, one of the many properties of the Thompson family.

Granday Canning Company and the Turtle Kraals.

The Thompsons were a power in the Keys. Charles's oldest brother, Norberg, was elected mayor of Key West in 1915. He also served on the city and county commissions, the Overseas Highway Committee and the Everglades National Park Commission. Brother Karl was the county sheriff from 1933 to 1941.

The three Thompson boys were all educated in the northeast. Norberg earned a law degree from New York University. Karl was a graduate of Amherst College in Massachusetts. Charles, who was born in 1899, a year earlier than Hemingway, attended New York City public schools and the Mount Pleasant Military School at Ossining-on-the-Hudson, New York, but not college. He just wasn't as smart as his brothers, but he was a much nicer man, recalls his old friend, Bill Gaiser. "The family recognized it and gave him a less complicated part of the business to run," said Gaiser.

A charter member of the Hemingway Mob, Thompson fished the waters of the Gulf of Mexico, Florida Bay and the Gulf Stream. When Hemingway traveled to Wyoming to hunt in the spring of 1932, Charles went with him. Both men bagged elks and grizzly bears. It proved to be a warmup for a much bigger expedition the following year.

In the fall of 1933 Charles joined Ernest and Pauline on the great African safari Hemingway had dreamed of for years. Once again Uncle Gus Pfeiffer, who had bought their car and their house for them, came through with the money for the nine-month trip—a fat $25,000. Charles paid his own way.

Thompson took a steamer from New York to Marseilles, then a train to Paris. There he was met by Ernest, wearing a black Basque beret and holding a magnum of champagne. The small-town hardware dealer was treated to a grand tour of Paris by a man whose knowledge of the French capital was encyclopedic. In the nearby countryside the two hunting buddies shot deer and pheasant.

On their final night in Paris, Ernest, Pauline and Charles played host to one of the world's most famous and controversial authors, the

Irishman James Joyce. Joyce had written *Ulysses*, an experimental novel too hot to make it past America's prudish censors. Charles, who had already caroused with such literary friends of Hemingway's as John Dos Passos, Archibald MacLeish and Maxwell Perkins, got drunk that night with the famous Irishman. He later described him as "a grand little man."

From Marseilles Charles and the Hemingways sailed to Africa. When they disembarked in sweltering heat in Mombasa, Kenya, Hemingway wore a wide-brimmed Stetson, Pauline an ankle-length white dress and Charles a suit and tie. "Pauline and I looked like missionaries," Charles later recalled. "...Ernest had the distinct look of a whiskey drummer."

The train to Nairobi took them past Mount Kilimanjaro. Ernest was so excited Charles said his grin was "plastered on his face." The excitement the mountain created would surface later in one of the author's most memorable short stories, "The Snows of Kilimanjaro."

For their safari they engaged the services of the most famous of all the African white hunters, Philip Percival. They would later be joined by Percival's partner, the Danish Baron Bror von Blixen, the husband of Isak Dinesen, who wrote *Out of Africa*.

Hemingway wrote his own book about his African adventures: *Green Hills of Africa*. In his book Pauline becomes P.O.M.—Poor Old Mama—and Charles emerges as Old Karl, a confusing move since Charles already had a brother named Karl.

From the start Thompson outshot Hemingway, not because he was trying to outshine his friend, but simply because he had better eyesight. They moved south to the Serengeti Plains and celebrated Christmas Day on the shores of Lake Eyasi. Finally Hemingway, after a number of lesser kills, shot a rhinoceros—only to learn that Charles had just killed one. In his safari book, he wrote: "We went over. There was the newly severed head of a rhino that was a rhino. He was twice the size of the one I had killed....He had made my rhino look so small that I could never keep him in the same small town where we lived."

Near the end of the hunt Hemingway killed two giant kudu bulls with magnificent horns at a salt lick near a Masai village. He had redeemed his reputation as a mighty hunter. He was able to bask in the glow of his triumph—at least for a short while. When he returned to camp, he learned that Charles had bagged one of the largest kudu heads ever taken in East Africa.

In his book Hemingway was generous in his praise of Charles: "I was, truly, very fond of him and he was entirely unselfish and altogether self-sacrificing." But, he lamented: "Why does he have to beat me so bloody badly."

Back home again the warm friendship between Charles and Ernest was soon to face a test far greater than the pressures of an African shootout. Late in December, 1936, Hemingway met the author and foreign correspondent Martha Gellhorn in Sloppy Joe's. That meeting would lead eventually to the breakup of Hemingway's second marriage.

As Ernest and Pauline drifted apart, Charles's wife, Lorine, became openly hostile to Ernest, and even Charles for a while became distant in his dealings with his old friend. The Thompsons were small-town, old-fashioned people. They didn't like divorce and they sided with Pauline and the children.

Ernest patched up his relationships with the Thompsons but not with Pauline. The marriage dragged on till Labor Day, 1940. Circuit Court Judge George "Kitty" Gomez had received a request to conduct a divorce proceeding on a holiday to avoid publicity. He couldn't believe it when he walked into his Miami courtroom and saw standing before him his old friends Charles and Lorine Thompson. He thought of them as "as happy a couple as ever married."

The Thompsons quickly explained that it was a divorce *in absentia*. They were simply standing in for the Hemingways. Later the judge joked about it with them, but they found nothing to laugh about.

On his occasional trips back to Key West from his new home in Cuba, the author continued to call on his old friends. His last visit to them was in 1960. Lorine recalled it: "He was coming through from Cuba on his way West. You know, he usually had a spring in his walk that sort of shook the whole house. But that time, his feet were sort of dragging."

A year later, in Ketchum, Idaho, Hemingway killed himself with a shotgun. Charles made one last visit to his old friend—to attend his funeral.

Charles died on February 18, 1978, in his rambling, rundown house on Seminary Street. His walls were still decorated with the heads of the trophy kills from the African safari, among them the giant kudu that had so embarrassed Hemingway—and Charles.

"It seemed so unfair," he recalled once. "Ernest was a better hunter and a better shot. But almost every time I shot something bigger. It was just a freak."

SLOPPY JOE

Their friendship was foreordained. Joe Russell had two things essential to Ernest Hemingway's happiness—a charter boat for fishing and a speakeasy for imbibing. If those two elements weren't enough, Josie did Hemingway a favor that endeared him to the author forever.

Not long after he arrived in Key West Ernest received a royalty check from Charles Scribner's for *A Farewell to Arms*. When the author took the check, for just under a thousand dollars, to the First National Bank, the bank president took one look at Hemingway and what did he see? A scruffy-looking bum. Definitely not the kind of man who should be bringing in a thousand-dollar check. Too big a risk. He refused to cash it.

Hemingway went next to Sloppy Joe's, Russell's tiny elbow-shaped speakeasy at the corner of Front and Duval streets. Without hesitation, Josie cashed the check for Ernest. It was a welcome gesture of trust. It also revealed Russell as a successful businessman with a good supply of cash on hand.

Hemingway promptly returned to the bank and told President William Porter, "To hell with your bank. I have my own private bank now and I'll get all my checks cashed there from now on."

Russell and Hemingway were fishing buddies from the start,

always comfortable with each other. Josie Grunts, as Ernest called him, was born in Key West in 1890. He had worked for a while as a cigarmaker until most of the industry moved away to Tampa. Later he opened a speakeasy and bought a boat big enough to fish the waters of the Gulf of Mexico, the Gulf Stream and the Atlantic.

Combining the enterprises of charter boating with the operation of an illegal saloon, Josie took a logical next step. Instead of buying bootleg whiskey for his speakeasy, he moved into the rumrunning business, in effect eliminating the middle man. Hemingway claimed that the red-faced Conch was the first Key Wester to make the run to Cuba to bring back Hoover Gold, as Josie called illegal booze.

Russell, who was married and had a son and two daughters,

Historical Association of Southern Florida

Sloppy Joe Russell raises a toast to a successful day's fishing with Hemingway.

behaved himself in Key West, seldom drinking in his hometown. The high seas and Havana were the two places where he cut loose.

He used to tell Hemingway about the fun of marlin fishing off Cuba. "Ernest," he said, "those big fish are the most exciting thing to catch there is."

In April of 1929 Hemingway chartered *Anita,* Josie's 34-foot, sponger-type launch, for half of Russell's usual fee of $20 a day for a trip to Cuba. The outing was planned for two weeks. It lasted two months.

They rented rooms at the Ambos Mundos Hotel in Havana for $2 a day. In the mornings they fished for marlin and in the afternoons Ernest worked on the galley proofs for *Death in the Afternoon.*

After dark the nightlife of Havana beckoned: jai alai, seafood, daiquiris and the Cuban capital's famed beauties. On his later visits Ernest had a particular favorite, one Jane Mason. He faced something of a complication with this affair. Jane was married to a friend of his, Grant Mason, a major investor in Pan American Airways.

Like Ernest an avid fisherman, Jane helped solve the problem of where to meet by coming to his room at the Ambos Mundos. He later claimed that she would climb through the transom in her eagerness to join him. Apparently, very few people believed this boast.

"Her grave beauty had a madonnalike quality accentuated by a middle part in smoothed-back blond hair," Ernest's brother Leicester wrote of her. "She had large eyes and fine features." Even 'Silent Cal' Coolidge, who seldom reacted to anything, reacted to her. He called her "the likeliest young lady ever to enter the White House." To President Coolidge likeliest meant most beautiful. He was not given to hyperbole.

The "madonnalike quality" that Leicester wrote of was an illusion. In Denis Brian's *The True Gen* a friend of Jane's says of her: "Jane Mason not only drank a bit, but was one of the wildest, hairiest, most drinking, wenching, sexy superwomen in the world...."

Hemingway, who once described Jane's wealthy husband, the handsome Grant, as a "twerp," contrasted the Masons' marriage with the Russells'. As that old gang of his grew older and more mature,

Ernest lamented over his difficulty in persuading members of his mob to join him in his ventures without their wives. He wrote to Dos Passos: "Mrs. Mason is almost as apt at going places without her husband as Mr. Josie is without his wife. But then Mrs. Mason has also had her husband for a long time too although Mr. Josie I believe there is no doubt has had his much much oftener as well as longer than Mr. Mason."

Florida Photographic Archives

Marlins were big losers to a group of happy and accomplished anglers, left to right, Jane Mason, Ernest Hemingway and Josie Russell.

Pauline knew of her husband's affair with Jane. In a pathetic attempt to hold on to Ernest she tried to imitate Jane's distinctive hair style, even going as far as dyeing her dark hair blonde.

On December 5, 1933, at 5:32 P.M., an event occurred that made Mr. Josie less available for trips to Cuba. The repeal of the Eighteenth Amendment to the United States Constitution ended Prohibition. Joe Russell promptly moved out of the illegal speakeasy business into the legal saloon game. He rented a larger bar, called the Blind Pig, from Isaac Wolkowsky for three dollars a week.

The Blind Pig, located on the south side of the 400 block

of Greene Street, was a wooden frame building, fully three times as large as the original Sloppy Joe's. Dark and narrow, the bar had no front door. It didn't need one. The bar never closed. Josie operated Sloppy Joe's as a rowdy fisherman's saloon. Hemingway enjoyed observing the "types" who brought the bar a bustling business.

When *Pilar* arrived in Key West the following spring, Ernest invited Josie to accompany him on the new boat's maiden voyage to their old Havana haunts. For the first time, Joe declined a Hemingway invitation to fish. He was serious about making a success of his new bar. He was serious in many ways where Sloppy Joe's was concerned. He and his bartenders were required to wear blue serge pants, a white shirt and a tie. Josie always wore a bow tie.

At Sloppy Joe's the price was right, at least by today's standards. Ten beers for a dollar, ten cents for a shot of gin, fifteen cents for a whiskey and thirty-five cents for the bar's highest priced drink, Scotch and soda. Hemingway, who drank Haig and Haig Pinch Bottle, got his for a quarter, perhaps a volume discount.

On May 5, 1937, Sloppy Joe's moved again, this time just a half block to the southeast corner of Greene and Duval Streets. Josie had balked when Wolkowsky decided to raise the rent a dollar a week. Then he learned that the old Victoria Restaurant building was available. Bigger and better constructed, it featured the longest bar in town. The time has come, Josie reasoned, to own, not rent. He bought the building for $2500. The move to the new location was spectacular, dramatic and crafty.

The lease with Wolkowsky had stated that Josie would have to leave behind the many bar appointments he had added in his four years at the Greene Street location. So Joe let the lease expire, figuring that when the clock struck midnight he was no longer beholden to the terms of the document.

Josie recruited a large and effective force of movers. Their pay that night was drinks on the house at the new bar. Just after midnight the clientele begin picking up furniture and appointments, including the bar, and carrying them the half block to the new Sloppy Joe's. They also carried their drinks, if unfinished.

"Every drunk in town just happened by," Josie's son-in-law, Bill Cates, told Hemingway when he returned from Spain, "and they carried the whole damn place down the street where they got set up for a night of free drinks."

"Only in Key West," replied Ernest. "Only in Key West."

Wolkowsky returned from a trip to find the building at 428 Greene Street a mere shell. He was furious, of course, but his building continued to prosper as a bar site, first as the Duval Club and later as Captain Tony's.

Josie's premier bartender was a three-hundred-pound black named Al Skinner, a man with, it was said, a "Louis Armstrong smile." Joe Russell, Jr., said of him: "Skinner was as strong as a mule, could drink like a horse. But he had manners, always put a napkin down with your drink, always there to light your cigarette."

Another regular recalled: "Big Skinner was also Joe's hatchet man if there was anything or anyone to take care of. If Josie didn't want somebody around, Big Skinner would make sure."

When Artist Erik Smith painted a 1933 picture of Sloppy Joe's, he included Josie, Hemingway—and Skinner. The painting still hangs on the walls at Sloppy Joe's.

A hideway in the back of the saloon, named the Club Room, was used for gambling. Hemingway once said; "I used to be co-owner of Sloppy Joe's, silent partner they call it. We had gambling in the back and that's where the real money is."

Joe offered music on Saturday nights. Musicians played for tips from the crowd and a quart of whiskey and a bucket of ice water from Josie.

In June of 1941 Josie and Ernest planned to travel from Havana to New York to meet Toby Bruce and Betty Moreno, the future Mrs. Toby Bruce, who was working in New York. They were scheduled to attend a heavyweight championship fight between Joe Louis and Billy Conn at Madison Square Garden.

While in Havana, Josie entered a Cuban hospital for minor surgery. During recovery he suddenly suffered either a heart attack or a stroke. Just fifty-one, he died unexpectedly at 3 A.M. in the hospital.

Photo by Joan McIver

Sloppy Joe's bustles with action at night.

Ernest called Toby: "I'm sorry I stood you up but Josie died yesterday."

To his wife Pauline, Hemingway wrote: "Losing Mr. Josie was no fun for Mr. Josie and I was riding with him somewhere in it all only should have protected him better and truly. Thought he always had so much sense and judgement and so I didn't worry. No good to write about."

Though he died in 1941, Joe Russell's name lives on in Key West, in neon at his bar, Sloppy Joe's.

TOBY

Some described him as a handyman, others a jack-of-all-trades. You might even call him a true Renaissance man. It was said that he could fix anything. Hemingway called him Tobes. Scholarly biographies of Hemingway usually list him as either Otto or T. Otto Bruce. His full name was Telly Otto Bruce. Luckily, his initials, T.O.B., gave him a comfortable escape from either Telly or Otto. He answered to the affectionate name Toby.

For the last three decades of his life Hemingway sustained an enduring relationship with Toby Bruce. Toby was Hemingway's chauffeur, secretary and the guardian of Ernest's one true and lasting love, the boat *Pilar.* He was a hunter and a fisherman and he was a movie actor. He was a carpenter and a cabinetmaker. He made the house on Whitehead Street livable, then protected it with a wall and finally added the first swimming pool ever built in the Keys. He bought Hemingway's cars for him. He even negotiated the purchase of the author's home in Cuba, then supervised the massive project to convert La Finca Vigia into a home where Hemingway could live and work. He wrote letters for Ernest, read galley proofs and even demonstrated his talent for drawing by designing the dust jacket for *For Whom the Bell Tolls.* After the author's death, he and his wife Betty worked with Ernest's widow, Mary, to sort out the vast assortment of Hemingway material found stored at Sloppy Joe's. Through it all Toby was a friend, who stayed close to Ernest through three marriages, starting with Pauline.

To Pauline, however, Toby was a servant. His home town was Piggott, Arkansas, where the Pfeiffers were the lords of the realm. Toby's father owned a hardware store and worked as a mule and horse trader. Toby, who was born June 24, 1910, met Ernest in 1928 on the author's first visit to Piggott, just prior to Patrick's birth in Kansas City. Ernest was walking along the street, wearing tattered clothes, with a ragged beard and a burn under one eye. One arm was in a sling. Jeering teenagers tossed rocks at him. They were surprised when he went to the home of Piggott's wealthiest family, and even more surprised when he was let in. The teenagers, afraid they had committed a massive blunder, asked Toby, who was only 18, to apologize for them. When he went to the Pfeiffers' home, he was introduced to the "tramp," who turned out to be Pauline's husband.

Toby and Ernest met again when Hemingway returned from Kansas City after Patrick was born. This time the sling was gone, so the two of them went trap shooting together. Two years later Toby supervised the refurbishing of the Whitehead Street home. In 1934 they hunted quail together and Ernest raised the possibility of Bruce coming back to Key West to build a brick wall around the Hemingway home. Toby hitchhiked to Key West in 1935, then stayed on the island most of the rest of his life.

Hemingway had good reason for wanting a wall. He had been furious ever since the city's tourism promoters had listed his house as Key West tourist attraction No. 18. He decided the best way to keep the sightseers at bay was to build a wall.

It was not a simple task. Toby had never built a brick wall and never before labored in Key West's summer heat. For his building blocks Toby hoped to use bricks dug up when the city decided to pave its streets with asphalt, a move that for some reason infuriated Hemingway. He sent Toby out at night to harvest "old Baltimore" bricks from their dump site and bring them back to the house in a borrowed pickup truck. One night Toby was caught in the act. Charging Toby and his illustrious accomplice with "grand theft bricks" would bring down unwelcome publicity on the island's most famous citizen. The matter was settled out-of-court. Hemingway agreed to pay a penny a brick.

Toby wasn't sure how good a job he'd done, but Ernest was delighted when the six-foot wall was completed in late August.

"Now that I've gone private," he said to Toby, "they might even take me off the tourist list." It was a split decision. Hemingway's house stayed on the tourist list but the wall gave him the privacy he had wanted. He set in immediately to read the galley proofs for *Green Hills of Africa.*

Toby's goal had been to complete the job before hurricane season, when loose building materials could become missiles. The wall finished, he set out for Piggott on August 30. Three days later the most devastating hurricane in Keys history, the Labor Day hurricane of 1935, hit the Upper Keys. He learned of the terrible storm when he visited a cousin in Evansville, Indiana.

On Toby's return to Key West Hemingway showed his pleasure with Bruce's work. "Went on the payroll fulltime in 1935," said Toby. "Ernest paid me $65 a week. Good wages back then."

And what did he do for his money? "Everything. Worked his fishing boat. Built his furniture. Took his glasses off when he'd fall asleep in bed. Drove his car on all his trips. Carried his money. Bought what he needed. Even read proof and corrected the spelling for *For Whom the Bell Tolls*."

Dust Jacket for
For Whom the Bell Tolls
was designed by Toby Bruce.

Photo by Stuart McIver

Drawing was another of Toby's many skills. Hemingway had him design the dust jacket for his book about the Spanish Civil War. Bruce sketched out a little village at the foot of a mountain. In the background is the bridge that was blown up. An artist at Scribner's did the finished artwork.

Toby treasured a leather-bound copy of the galley-proof sheets. Hemingway had inscribed the book to him:

"With much affection and deep appreciation for all he did to make this book—Ernest Hemingway."

When Papa moved away to Cuba, Toby went with him, rejecting Pauline's efforts to hire him. Hemingway felt his celebrity status would drive up the price of the property he and Martha Gellhorn wanted to buy, so Toby handled the purchase, keeping the famous author out of the proceedings.

Bruce kept in touch with Key West, particularly with one Laura Elizabeth "Betty" Moreno. Pretty Betty, good-natured but feisty, traced her Key West lineage back to her great-grandfather, Benjamin Curry, before the Civil War. She knew Hemingway from the days when he had briefly rented a house across the street from her family home. As a child, she played with Ernest's oldest son, Jack, better known as Bumby, when he visited his father. "He was a beautiful boy," she recalls of Hemingway's son from his first marriage.

When World War II came, Toby returned to the United States. He worked with the Army Corps of Engineers in California and Betty took a job as an assembler with Sperry Gyroscope in Brooklyn. They married in New York in 1943.

After the war the Bruces returned to Key West. Toby opened the Home Appliance Store, an enterprise that made good use of his reputation as a fix-anything man. He continued to visit Hemingway in Cuba and the Bruces saw him too on his occasional trips back to Key West.

One day at the beach Betty made friends with a visiting couple. She gave them a tour of Key West, then took them to meet some of her friends. When she introduced him as Bud Schubert, he corrected her.

"It's Budd Schulberg," he said.

The author of the acclaimed novel *What Makes Sammy Run* and of the screenplay for the Oscar-winning movie "On the Waterfront." Schulberg became a close friend of the Bruce family.

Soon, Budd was hard at work on another screenplay, this one for "Wind Across the Everglades," a tale of plume-hunting days in Florida. Christopher Plummer was cast in the role of the Audubon warden who tries to stop the illegal slaughter of the egrets, whose feathers were used to decorate women's hats. Burl Ives played the role of Cottonmouth, head of a nefarious gang of poachers portrayed by such diverse performers as heavyweight boxer Tony Galento, jockey Sammy Renick, clown Emmett Kelly and actor Peter Falk, the future Columbo. Stripper Gypsy Rose Lee was cast as a whorehouse madam and author MacKinley Kantor as a judge.

Schulberg asked Toby what part he would like. He said he would like to be a bootlegger. So the scriptwriter wrote in the part for him. In the acknowledgments for the book version of the film, shot mostly in Everglades City, Schulberg wrote: "...my old fishing and

Matusa-rum drinking chum from Key West, Toby Bruce, made his cinematic debut as Joe Bottles."

Budd must have liked Toby's work. For his next film, "A Face in the Crowd," shot in Piggott, Arkansas, he employed Toby as a technical advisor. The movie featured Andy Griffith in the starring role.

Toby's film work with Schulberg clearly qualified him to evaluate another great actor. "He was one of the greatest actors I've ever known," he said of Papa. "Nobody has ever been able to play Hemingway the way Ernest did. And they never will."

AND A FOE–THE KINGFISH

The little island of Key West seems hardly large enough to accommodate the two enormous egos that occupied space there in the mid-1930s. One bristled within the hefty frame of an author whose distaste for tourism has not prevented his unforgettable name from becoming totally entwined with the city's latter-day travel trade. The other lived within the arrogant heart of a powerful government official who saved a dying town by transforming it into a tourist's dream and today is almost forgotten in the city he created.

Ernest Hemingway and Julius F. Stone, Jr., two of the most powerful men on the island, were not friends. They had a few things in common, such as remarkable intelligence and mighty wills. They were close to each other in age and both had midwestern roots. Stone hailed from Columbus, Ohio; Hemingway from Oak Park, Illinois. On a personal level each man was used to having his own way. Each could be high-handed and abrasive in his dealings with people, although Ernest wielded a large measure of charm much of the time.

Apart from the chemistry problem, the major clash appears to have been political. Hemingway was raised in a conservative midwestern Republican home. He favored as little government as possible. Stone, on the other hand, was a zealous New Deal Democrat, convinced that government could fix society's problems. As far as Key West was concerned, it turned out that the irritating Stone was right, which probably rankled Hemingway even more.

Stone came to the island in 1934 after a call for help from Florida's governor, David L. Sholtz. The governor had officially declared the bankrupt island a welfare state. Paying jobs were scarce. The cigar and sponge industries had both moved to the Tampa Bay area. The Navy, a fixture since 1832, abandoned its Key West base a century later as did the Coast Guard. Mallory Steamship Lines no longer called at the island, and Henry Flagler's Florida East Coast Railway was in bankruptcy. Its tax base shattered, Key West, once Florida's most affluent city, had sunk five million dollars into debt. The city was unable to pay policemen, firemen and garbage collectors. Eighty per cent of its residents were on welfare. Per capita income was down to $7 a month. No wonder Hemingway called it "the St. Tropez of the poor."

As southeastern director of the Federal Emergency Relief Administration (FERA), Julius Stone faced the problem of what to do about Key West. Something about the Key West mission appealed mightily to Stone. Possibly it was the lure of unlimited power, or maybe the challenge of reviving what had once been America's most prosperous city.

Stone saw abandoned buildings and houses, collapsing piers, streets littered with garbage. He began by organizing relief recipients into the Key West Volunteer Corps, telling them: "Your city is bankrupt, your streets are littered and filthy, your homes are rundown and your industry is gone. We will begin by cleaning up, then we will rebuild." Among his 4,000 volunteers was a man of 102.

The Kingfish pondered his options. With $2.5 million he could provide relief, including food and medical care for the needy, for five years. But the problem would remain: no jobs, no tax base.

Another option discussed was simply to close down the island and relocate some three thousand families to the mainland, probably Tampa, where there was some hope of jobs. Not workable, he concluded.

The third was to find some way to rehabilitate the island. The

Kingfish gazed out over his realm, and looked past garbage and rundown houses. This time he saw azure waters teeming with fish, brilliant sunsets over the Gulf of Mexico, bougainvillea in bloom and distinctive architecture. He heard the rustle of the trade winds through the coconut palms. The answer jumped out at him: Transform Key West into a tourist resort, a touch of the tropics in a temperate zone.

He put his volunteers to work painting and repairing houses. He even made the renovation pay for itself. The owners retained title to their houses but the Key West Administration rented them out and applied the rent money to the cost of renovation. After the costs were paid off, the rent money then went to the owners.

Nothing in the FERA guidelines provided for his free-wheeling deals, but that didn't slow him down. "I got away with it," he told *The New Yorker* magazine years later, "because we were so far off no one knew what we were doing." Stone reveled in the power the job gave him: "With a scratch of my pen I started this work in Key West, and with a scratch of my pen I can stop it—just like that."

In five months, from July to mid-December, 1935, Stone's volunteers renovated more than two hundred guest houses, built thatched huts on the beach, painted and cleaned restaurants, bars and nightclubs and remodeled the once-elegant Casa Marina Hotel, which had slipped into receivership. Streets were landscaped and a municipal sewer system followed demolition of the town's outhouses. On Mallory Square FERA built the Key West Aquarium. Work resumed on the Overseas Highway, and an airline was subsidized to serve a repaired and improved airport. The Kingfish enriched the cultural life of the island by bringing in artists and organizing theater and choral groups.

Stone made sure the nation's press knew about the Key West story. Within a year the improvement was spectacular. In 1935 40,000 tourists came to Key West. The island's hotels reported an 85 percent increase in guests. Passenger travel into the city increased 42.5 percent. Unemployment was reduced by two-thirds.

Not everything went smoothly. To further his goal of a "tropical

Bermuda," Stone began wearing Bermuda shorts to work, hoping to encourage others to follow his lead. Reaction came quickly. One day an individualistic islander showed up for work in his drawers: "If Julius Stone can come to work in his underwear, so can I."

Monroe County Library

Julius Stone, at right, and J.J. Trevor, president of the First National Bank, stand in front of the East Martello Towers Museum and Art Gallery. Its doors were given to the museum by the bank and gratefully accepted by the Kingfish as president of the Key West Art and Historical Society.

The conservative *Florida Grower,* published in Orlando, wrote: "FERA rule is the rule of fear. No American city is more completely ruled by one man than is this small island city." In the United Press Harry Ferguson called Stone "the king of a tight little empire....Call it a 'dictatorship,' a 'kingdom within a republic,' or anything you choose."

Hemingway was particularly irritated by a map prepared by FERA, listing forty-eight sights for a tourist to see in Key West. It included such memorable attractions as the Sponge Lofts, the Ice Factory, the new Tropical Open Air Aquarium and the Turtle Crawl, owned by Charles Thompson's family. Number eighteen in the list was

Hemingway's home. Gawkers trying to peer into his home disturbed him so much he hired Toby Bruce to build a six-foot brick wall around his place. In a piece called "The Sights of Whitehead Street: A Key West Letter" in *Esquire* he even reported that tourists, thinking they were visiting an official attraction, occasionally walked right into his home.

Hemingway's wrath showed in a letter in which he referred to Stone as "that damned Jew administrator" and in numerous references in *To Have and Have Not.* One of the characters in his Key West novel sees an unattractive woman and comments "Anyone would have to be a writer or a FERA man to have a wife like that." Another character complains that Conchs cannot eat "working here in Key West for the government for six and a half (dollars) a week," overlooking the fact that before Stone's arrival the average per capita income was seven dollars a month.

The heavy hand of Stone's administration was too much for Hemingway. Even with solid accomplishments Stone was unable to overcome Ernest's opposition to government intrusion. There is a degree of selfishness, too, in the author's attitude. He was opposed to tourism because an obscure, rundown town gave him more freedom to work. The plight of Conchs out of work seems not to have touched him, perhaps because he knew no want himself. After all, he had married a rich woman.

Stone moved on in 1937 to study law at Harvard University, where he had previously earned a Ph.D. in organic chemistry. He would later return to Key West and practice law on such a free-wheeling basis that he had to flee the country to escape prosecution. Like Hemingway, he lived for a while in Cuba, but there is no indication that their paths crossed there. Both, however, had to flee the island when Castro came into power. Stone died in 1967 in New South Wales, Australia.

Even after their deaths in the 1960s the lives of these two monstrous egos continued to be intertwined. Stone, to Hemingway's dismay, had converted Key West into a tourism destination. It was moving up in popularity when World War II intervened. After the war it became a vacation home for President Harry Truman, who made

Americans even more aware of the city at the end of the Keys. It remained, ironically, the posthumous fate of Ernest Hemingway, who loathed tourists, to fulfill Julius Stone's dream of making Key West one of America's best known tourist destinations.

CHAPTER VII

❖ ❖ ❖ ❖ ❖ ❖ ❖ ❖ ❖ ❖ ❖

HEMINGWAY'S HURRICANE

PAPA HEMINGWAY FIRST HEARD ABOUT THE STORM on Saturday night. He was sitting on the porch, having a drink and reading the evening paper. East of Long Island in the Bahamas, the hurricane on its current track was headed toward the Keys. It was news that was just alarming enough to disrupt his routine, but not quite alarming enough for panic.

Hemingway studied his storm chart, showing tracks and dates of forty September hurricanes since 1900. Using the speed of the storm in the Weather Bureau Advisory, he calculated the probable arrival time for the storm. No sooner than noon Monday, if it hit Key West at all.

Though he was an early riser, the next morning he found a line of boat owners already ahead of him, waiting to have their boats hauled out on the ways, an inclined structure for launching boats. He had to settle for $52 worth of heavy hawser to tie down *Pilar* in what he thought would be the safest part of the submarine base. He secured his boat before he turned his attention to his home.

On the morning of Labor Day, 1935, the *Miami Herald*, quoting the U.S. Weather Bureau, referred to the storm only as a "tropical disturbance." Still, it was clear enough by now that the time had come to board up the house. This was not just a "tropical disturbance." This was clearly a hurricane. Hemingway and his help nailed up the hurricane shutters and moved outside furniture into the house. By 5 o'clock that afternoon the wind was blowing hard and steadily from the northeast.

Ernest checked on his boat again, alarmed now that the Coast Guard had tied up a confiscated booze boat next to *Pilar.*

"For Christ's sake, you know those lousy ringbolts will pull out of her stern and then she'll come down on us."

"If she does, you can cut her loose or sink her."

"Sure, and maybe we can't get to her, too. What's the use of letting a piece of junk like that sink a good boat?"

Back on Whitehead Street the Hemingways hunkered down. Ernest figured the storm would hit at midnight. He tried to get a little sleep, placing a barometer and a flashlight by his bed to prepare for the inevitable loss of electricity. At midnight the wind was howling and the barometer had dropped to 29.55. He got up and dressed, then decided to go check on *Pilar.* His car wouldn't start, drowned out by the sheets of rain. On his way to the sub yard Hemingway's flashlight shorted out. When he reached the Navy yard, he saw the problem he had feared. The storm had blown the booze boat's ringbolts out. But the day was saved when a Spanish sailor, Jose Rodriguez, stepped in quickly and maneuvered the boat away from Ernest's craft.

What a storm! Ernest brooded. "You feel like hell," he wrote....

"You figure if we get the hurricane from there (the northwest) you will lose the boat and you will never have enough money to get another."

Monument to victims of the 1935 hurricane, in Islamorada.

Photo by Stuart McIver

By 2 o'clock he noticed a change. The worst of the winds had passed. By 5 o'clock the barometer was beginning to hold steady. Ernest began to work his way back home in the darkness just before the dawn. He found a tree across the walkway to his house. He noticed a strange empty look in his front yard, and then he saw the reason. The old sapodilla tree had blown down.

Pilar had weathered the storm and except for a few lost trees and branches, his property on Whitehead Street had come through in good shape. It was time to turn in.

The next day, a Tuesday, Key West was an isolated world. No communication with the outside world, no boats able to get in or out, no trains able to make it down the FEC tracks.

On Wednesday a boat from Key West finally reached Matecumbe Key. The news it brought back was horrifying. The hurricane was a small one with an eye only ten miles across. But it proved to be the most intense hurricane ever to strike the western hemisphere. Barometric pressure dropped to 26.35 inches, the lowest reading ever recorded. Wind gauges blew away. Estimates put the wind velocity at 250 miles per hour. A wall of water eighteen feet high swept over Matecumbe Key. Thirty five miles of railroad tracks were washed away. No train would ever again reach Key West.

It was not, however, the destruction of property that sickened the Conchs. The loss of life was staggering: nearly six hundred fatalities. Whole extended families of old-time Conchs were wiped out. Even more shocking to the nation was the death of some two hundred veterans of World War I. The men had been given temporary relief jobs working on the Overseas Highway that would one day connect Key West with the mainland. The death of the veterans infuriated Hemingway and led to one of the angriest pieces of writing he ever composed.

Hemingway had gotten to know some of the men in the bars of Key West. The veterans were a mixture: some damaged mentally, emotionally and physically by the war, others just Americans unable to find a job in the depths of the worst depression the country had ever known. The one thing they all had in common was service in World

War I, a duty that Hemingway respected deeply.

As soon as the seas would permit, Papa recruited Bra Saunders and Sully Sullivan as crew for a trip up to Islamorada to see for himself. "When we reached Lower Matecumbe there were bodies floating in the ferry slip," he wrote "...The biggest bunch of the dead were in the tangled, always green but now brown, mangroves behind the tank cars and the water towers. They hung on there, in shelter, until the wind and the rising water carried them away....Then further on you found them high in the trees where the water had swept them. You found them everywhere and in the sun all of them were beginning to be too big for their blue jeans and jackets that they could never fill when they were on the bum and hungry."

As he wrote, Hemingway was hurting for victims he knew personally, people like "two damned nice girls who ran a sandwich place and filling station." The author, no friend of the New Deal, blamed the government with such questions as "Who sent them down to the Florida Keys and left them there in hurricane months?" He implied that they were placed in harm's way because they were politically embarrassing.

Actually, confusion, blunder and incompetency were the enemies of the veterans, not an evil conspiracy. Hurricane forecasting had not come of age. Not even the Weather Bureau knew how terrible the storm would be. An evacuation plan had been in place to move the veterans out in an emergency, but the train to be used was not available until too late.

The final twist to his story was his choice of the publication for his work. The story was published on September 17, 1935, in *The New Masses*, a publication of the American Communist Party. The magazine had contacted him to write the piece and he agreed. He did not particularly like the publication, but it met a need. Ernest Hemingway, angry young man, had a story he had to get off his chest.

CHAPTER VIII

❖ ❖ ❖ ❖ ❖ ❖ ❖ ❖ ❖ ❖ ❖

THE KEY WEST BOOK

HEMINGWAY SPENT VERY LITTLE of his adult life in the country of his birth. He wrote a number of superb short stories set in America, many of them in Michigan where he spent his summers, but he wrote just one novel about life in the United States. For that novel he picked as his book's setting what is probably the most unrepresentative city in America. Key West is just not like any other place. He wrote about it simply because it was the one town he knew about.

Estate of Leicester Hemingway

Ernest Hemingway takes time off from work to relax on his patio.

He called his Key West book *To Have and Have Not,* a title reflecting a relevant theme in those Depression years. It was not one of his best books, which was unfortunate since Key West was a locale in which he spent a productive decade, writing all or parts of several books and some of his best short stories.

The book is at its best when capturing the look and the feel of Key West during troubled times. Hemingway depicts the life of struggling commercial fishermen, charterboat operators, saloonkeepers and veterans working on relief projects in the Keys.

In one passage he shows us nighttime Key West through the eyes of an unsympathetic character, novelist Richard Gordon:

"The moon was up now and the trees were dark against it, and he passed the frame houses with their narrow yards, light coming from the shuttered windows; the unpaved alleys, with their double rows of houses; Conch town, where all was starched, well-shuttered, virtue, failure, grits and boiled grunts, undernourishment, prejudice, righteousness, interbreeding and the comforts of religion; the open doored, lighted Cuban bolito houses, shacks whose only romance was their names; the Red House, Chicha's; the pressed stone church; its steeples sharp, ugly triangles against the moonlight; the big grounds and the long, black-domed bulk of the convent, handsome in the moonlight; a filling station and a sandwich place, bright-lighted beside a vacant lot where a miniature golf course had been taken out; past the brightly lit main street with the three drug stores, the music store, the five Jew stores, three pool-rooms, two barbershops, five beer joints, three ice cream parlors, the five poor and the one good restaurant, two magazine and paper places, four second-hand joints (one of which made keys), a photographer's, an office building with four dentists' offices upstairs, the big dime store, a hotel on the corner with taxis opposite; and across, behind the hotel, to the street that led to jungle town, the big unpainted frame house with lights and the girls in the doorway, the mechanical piano going, and a sailor sitting in the street; and then on back, past the back of the brick courthouse with its clock luminous at half-past ten, past the whitewashed jail building shining in the moonlight, to the embowered entrance of the Lilac Time where motor cars filled the alley."

Hemingway's hero was Harry Morgan, a charterboat captain at a time when the Great Depression dragged the deep sea fishing business down into the depths. A series of cruel breaks force him to resort to such illegal ventures as rumrunning and smuggling of aliens.

In *To Have and Have Not* Hemingway drew so heavily on real people that a fear of libel suits induced him to invite Arnold Gingrich and the Scribner's lawyer, Maurice "Moe" Speiser, to join him in Key West. They reviewed the manuscript for possible trouble spots.

Gingrich, the editor of *Esquire*, was the man who had suggested that Hemingway write the novel. Ernest had already written two long short stories about Harry Morgan, one of which ran in *Esquire*, the other in *Cosmopolitan*. By adding a third long story and weaving them together, Hemingway could fashion a short novel, reasoned Gingrich. Unfortunately, the three separate pieces never quite came together.

When he read the completed manuscript, Gingrich felt an uncomfortable jolt. One of the characters, the novelist James MacWhalsey, was based somewhat on Gingrich, no particular problem since the portrait is actually a likeable one. The problem lay with the character Helene Bradley, clearly patterned on Jane Mason.

At Bimini Hemingway had introduced Arnold to the beauteous Jane. Within a few months a smitten Gingrich was seeing her secretly in New York; eventually, after Jane divorced Grant Mason, she and Arnold married. Arnold suggested to Ernest that Jane and Grant Mason were being "libeled right up to their eyebrows."

"Goddam editor comes down to Bimini and sees a blonde and he hasn't been the same since," teased Hemingway, who obviously knew of the affair.

In the final section that Ernest had written, Grant Mason is depicted as Tommy Bradley, an impotent playboy, and Jane as his nymphomaniac wife, Helene, who collects writers. Since Bradley can't satisfy Helene, he leaves her free to sport with anyone she wishes as long as he gets to watch on occasion.

This would not have made for easy reading for Gingrich. The Scribner's attorney was not happy with it either. He insisted on a strong, though clearly untrue, disclaimer in the front of the book: "In view of a recent tendency to identify characters in fiction with real people, it seems proper to state that there are no real people in this volume: both the characters and their names are fictitous. If the name of any living person has been used, the use was purely accidental."

In addition, Gingrich's remarks were heeded to some extent. Some passages were slightly sanitized. Still, the disclaimer didn't fool either the Conchs or the literary critics. It became a popular pastime to figure out who the characters were in real life.

In his *Papa: Hemingway in Key West*, author James McLendon presents his rogues' gallery of characters. The book's lead, Harry Morgan, a name adopted from the famed English pirate, was based loosely on Josie Russell, who works overtime as the additional inspiration for Freddy Wallace, the owner of Freddy's Bar, which of course is Sloppy Joe's. Harry's boat, *Queen Conch*, is Josie's *Anita*. Eddy Marshall, a rummy who serves as Harry's first mate, was based on Joe Lowe, a local fisherman killed in the 1935 hurricane.

The Key West states attorney, George Brooks, whom Hemingway met on his first day in Key West, becomes Bee-Lips, also an attorney. The strange nickname grew out of the way he wrapped his lips around a cigarette.

Captain Bra Saunders appears in the book as charterboat captain Willie Adams, a crusty but sympathetic character, "an old man in a felt hat and a windbreaker."

Captain Willie tries to protect Harry from the wrath of Frederick Harrison, a stiff, arrogant, insensitive government administrator. Harrison swears out an affidavit that deprives Morgan of the boat he needs to make a living. When he describes himself as "one of the three most important men in the United States today," it seems clear enough that Ernest is throwing a barb at Julius Stone, the high-handed "Kingfish" of Key West.

An unflattering portrait of a writer named James Laughlin and his wife was based on Mr. and Mrs. Jack Coles, friends of John Dos Passos. By now the friendship between Dos Passos and Hemingway was beginning to collapse. Ernest had difficulty when writer-friends achieved high success. At a time when Hemingway's reviews were less than complementary, Dos Passos was drawing raves for his *The Big Money*, part two in what would eventually become his classic trilogy, *U.S.A.* Acclaim which particularly galled Hemingway was a glowing cover story in *Time* magazine. Only four other American authors had

had their pictures on the cover of *Time.*

Ernest struck back at his old friend by basing the character Richard Gordon on Dos Passos. Gordon is presented as a successful but shallow novelist, one of the writers ensnared by the charms—and the availability—of Helene. Unfortunately, Tommy peeks in to watch them in the act and Richard, understandably, goes limp. When he stops, Helene slaps him twice, then snarls: "So that's the kind of man you are. I thought you were a man of the world. Get out of here."

Gordon's wife Helen decides to break up with him and hurls at him what was meant to be a withering insult: "You writer." Was it Dos Passos being insulted? Or was it a case of self-loathing? Could Hemingway really have liked what he was doing to a man who had been a good friend before he became too successful in Hemingway's chosen field?

Ernest had become an unhappy man. His marriage was falling apart and his recent books had been poorly received by many critics. He disliked what the New Deal was doing to his Florida Keys, and he was shaken by events in his beloved Spain. There the Fascists he hated were seeking to overthrow the country's first democratic government.

Jeffrey Lynn, author of *Hemingway*, a biography that won the Los Angeles Times Book Award, identifies Helen as a somewhat disguised Pauline. In *To Have and Have Not* Helen is a Catholic, as was Pauline, and she speaks with abhorrence of birth control devices and abortion. Hers is a troubled Catholic conscience and hers is the withering "You writer." Who knows what frictions were developing in the Hemingways' marriage? What is known is that the marriage was beginning to unravel and a terrible sadness was beginning to claim both of them.

It is ironic that *To Have and Have Not,* Hemingway's only book set in Key West, turned out to be one of his lesser works. His time on the island was actually one of his most productive periods. While living in Key West, he completed one of his greatest novels, *A Farewell to Arms,* and started another major work, *For Whom The Bell Tolls.* He wrote his bullfighting opus, *Death in the Afternoon,* and *Green Hills of Africa,* a novelized account of his safari. Hemingway even brought the Spanish Civil War to Key West, where he completed revisions on *The Fifth Column*, his only play, and worked on the script for a documentary film, *The Spanish Earth*. Among the short stories he wrote in Key West were "The Short Happy Life of Francis Macomber," "The Snows of Kilimanjaro" and "A Way You'll Never Be," a Nick Adams story. He used an account Captain Bra told him about the shipwreck of the Spanish liner, *Val Banera*, as a springboard for "After the Storm," his first story based in Florida.

Two of the books Hemingway wrote in Key West.

Photo by Stuart McIver

From his experiences and contacts in Key West he drew inspiration for a book that he would not write until the early 1950s. In the Dry Tortugas, McLendon writes, Ernest observed Bra Saunders' gnarled hands beginning to freeze up on him. He saw the sadness in the old fisherman's eyes as he faced the day when his hands would no longer work for him. Two decades later these hands, concludes McLendon, would become the hands of Santiago, an old Cuban fisherman, whose character was based on two Hispanic boatmen Ernest first met in his Key West years—Carlos Gutierrez and Gregorio Fuentes. *The Old Man and the Sea*, Santiago's story, would emerge as one of the best of all Hemingway's novels, reclaiming for him his lofty perch in the world of letters. The book won for him the 1953 Pulitzer Prize and contributed strongly to the Nobel Prize he won in 1954 "for his mastery of the art of narrative, most recently demonstrated in *The Old Man and the Sea*, and for the influence that he has exerted on contemporary style."

❖

CHAPTER IX

❖ ❖ ❖ ❖ ❖ ❖ ❖ ❖ ❖ ❖ ❖

PAULINE AND THE BOYS

KEY WEST BELONGED to Hemingway, first in the 30s when he lived there and then again after his death in 1961. But there was a period after he left and moved to Cuba when the Hemingway the island took to its heart was not Ernest but rather Pauline. When their marriage finally broke apart, it was Pauline the Conchs sided with. Long after he left she stayed on in Key West, operating a business, maintaining the house and, most important of all, raising their children.

Pauline Pfeiffer, who was four years older than Ernest, grew up in the small rural town of Piggott, in the far northeastern corner of Arkansas, not far from St. Louis, where the Pfeiffers hailed from. Her family became the power structure of Piggott. Paul Pfeiffer, her father, who had made a small fortune with a chain of drug stores, owned sixty thousand acres of farmland, the cotton gin and the bank in Piggott. Her uncles in St. Louis, among them the generous Gus, owned the controlling interest in the Richard Hudnut Company, a cosmetics and pharmaceuticals company which included among its products the well-known rub Sloan's Liniment. She was raised in an intensely religious atmosphere. Her mother was a devout Catholic, and the Pfeiffer's sprawling white frame house included a chapel.

The future Mrs. Hemingway majored in journalism at the University of Missouri, then went to work on newspapers in Cleveland and New York before becoming a fashion reporter for *Vanity Fair* magazine. Her next move was to Paris where her fashion writing skills led to the post of assistant to the editor of *Vogue.* In Paris she met Ernest. He was married at the time to Hadley Richardson, the first of his four wives.

Pauline was attracted to the tall, handsome and already famous writer she saw in the cafés of Montparnasse. He in turn began to notice the slender, shapely woman with dark brown, sometimes impish eyes and stylishly bobbed hair. The attraction grew into a love affair that was painful for both of them. All his life Hemingway held a deep love for Hadley, and Pauline, a friend of Hadley's, was a devoutly religious woman. She regarded extramarital sex as a sin, made even worse by adultery.

In January, 1927, Hadley divorced Hemingway on grounds of desertion. Ernest and Pauline were married on May 10 in a Catholic ceremony in the fashionable Parisian church of St-Honore-d'Eykau in the Place Victor-Hugo. Raised as a Congregationalist, Hemingway now professed to be a Catholic, using questionable claims to satisfy the qualms of the church. In time, he would become what some Key West friends called a good Catholic.

The bride, always stylish, wore a silk dress and a single strand of pearls. She induced the ofttimes casual groom to wear a three-piece tweed suit and button-down shirt.

By the time they first set foot in Key West a year later, Pauline was already pregnant. On her first visit she met Lorine Thompson, Charles's wife, who would remain one of her closest friends for the rest of her life. Pauline did not want her baby born on a run-down tropical island. The Hemingways headed west and on June 27, 1928, labor pains sent Pauline to Research Hospital in Kansas City. Eighteen hours later the nine-and-a-half-pound Patrick was born by Caesarean section. It was a difficult labor, so difficult that her doctor warned that she must not become pregnant again for at least three years.

Just a little over three years later Pauline returned to Research Hospital for the birth of her second child. Again a long and difficult labor, again Caesarian section. The nine-pound baby was named Gregory Hancock Hemingway. He was the third son of the author. Unfortunately, Ernest had wanted a daughter, "a little Pilar," as Pauline once put it.

Pauline was still weak when the Hemingways started the

fourteen-hundred-mile trip back to Key West. They moved into the house at 907 Whitehead Street just six days before Christmas, 1931. The house was a mess. As Christmas approached, the house was crawling with workers, struggling valiantly to make the house livable.

Young Patrick, aged three, created true chaos. He mixed a toxic potion in a spray can and then sprayed the baby. Crisis number one. Crisis number two followed when he ate an ant-repellent pellet laced with arsenic. He vomited for the next twenty-four hours. In the confusion that followed, Patrick's French nurse, Gabrielle, became sick and Ernest developed a severe sore throat. Merry Christmas at Whitehead Street.

Isabelle, a spirited black woman, was hired to cook the meals that Ernest, always a zestful eater, needed for his energetic lifestyle. Ada Stern, an aptly named disciplinarian from Syracuse, New York, was engaged as housekeeper and placed in charge of the boys. Gregory has called her "an odd sort of Prussian governess."

Monroe County Library

Young Gregory Hemingway and housekeeper Ada Stern, a tough disciplinarian for the Hemingway sons.

When Patrick was seven, Ernest took him to St. Joseph's School, a large wooden school on Simonton Street, where he started first grade. Two years later Gregory would enter the same school.

Once, after Hemingway had returned from Spain, Gregory

showed him *Ferdinand the Bull*, a children's book that particularly delighted him. "That goddam kids' book has made ten times more than *Death in the Afternoon*," said Ernest. "I worked harder on *Death in the Afternoon* than on any other book in my life and that jerk who wrote *Ferdinand* might have spent a month on it."

In the fall of 1936 Patrick, age eight, and Gregory, age five, painted two of the Hemingway cats green. Toby tried to clean them up but failed. Both cats died. A furious Papa threatened to paint the boys green. For a week they hid from their father.

Arthur Valladares, whose father owned the town's principal book store, played with the boys after school. He particularly enjoyed romping in their swimming pool. Young Arthur was on good terms with Ernest. He delivered his New York newspapers to him.

The boys were not raised in the happiest of homes. By the mid-thirties their parents were moving inexorably toward the divorce that

Kennedy Library Collection

Hemingway with sons Patrick and John.

finally came in 1940. Old-fashioned, small-town people, the islanders generally sided with Pauline. They didn't favor such high-society concepts as breaking up a family with small children.

After the divorce, Pauline continued to live in Key West. She and Lorine Thompson went into business together, operating a drapery and upholstering store on Caroline Street.

In 1947 Patrick and Gregory were involved in an automobile accident in a small Crosley car that Pauline owned. Patrick bumped his head, but the injury did not appear to be serious. Soon after the accident he visited his father in Cuba. There at La Finca Vigia, Hemingway's home, he went into a violent delirium. Ernest personally cared for his son, helping him eat and sleeping just outside his room in the event of troubles during the night. Three months elapsed before he finally recovered.

Patrick would later move to Tanganyika where he owned a three-thousand-acre range. In time he would become a professional white hunter, a calling his father wrote about in books and short stories.

Gregory would eventually study medicine at the University of Miami and go on to pursue a medical career. For a while, though, he had to work his way through serious problems. In the summer of 1951 he was living in Southern California and working in an aircraft factory. A drug problem led to his arrest. His mother, in San Francisco at the time, flew down to Los Angeles to try to help him. That night she telephoned Ernest from the home of her sister, Ginny. His sarcastic remarks unhinged her. She broke into shouting and sobbing at his unsympathetic attitude.

That night she awoke at 1 o'clock with severe abdominal pain. Three hours later she died on the operating table at St. Vincent's Hospital. She was just 56. Ernest wrote Charles Scribner: "I loved her very much for many years and the hell with her faults."

Some months later Gregory visited his father in Cuba. When his son mentioned the arrest, Ernest said, "Well, it killed your mother."

After medical school, Gregory obtained a copy of Pauline's

autopsy. He learned that she had died of a rare tumor of the adrenal gland which had "fired off" apparently due not to the arrest but, Gregory believed, to the stress of the savage phone conversation. He wrote his father, presenting his side of the story, but the two never saw each other again.

CHAPTER X

❖ ❖ ❖ ❖ ❖ ❖ ❖ ❖ ❖ ❖ ❖

FAREWELL TO KEY WEST

IN LATE DECEMBER, 1936, Charles and Lorine Thompson arrived at Whitehead Street for dinner with Ernest and Pauline. It was a perfect Key West evening: soothing breeze off the ocean, seventy-degree temperature. Pauline, though, was uneasy with the drift of things. For one thing she was worried about the North American Newspaper Alliance's offer to Ernest. NANA wanted him to cover the war in Spain for the news service, a task that would not only place him in harm's way but at the very least remove him from Key West for long periods just as she was struggling to hold their marriage together.

She and the Thompsons relaxed with drinks until 7:30, the usual dinner hour. Pauline, clearly edgy, said: "Oh, Charles, you know where he is. Drag him back here and let's eat."

Charles knew exactly where Hemingway was. He drove his yellow Ford sedan down to Sloppy Joe's. Charles was unable, however, to persuade Ernest to leave. He returned to the Hemingway home and told Pauline: "He's talking to a beautiful blonde in a black dress. Says he'll meet us later at Pena's."

The plan had always been to enjoy an excellent Florida lobster dinner prepared with high skill by cook Miriam Williams and then to adjourn to Pena's Garden of Roses, a Key West beer garden. Pauline was not particularly concerned, but then she hadn't seen the beautiful blonde. That happened at Pena's when Ernest introduced her to Martha Gellhorn, a novelist, a journalist and, most dangerous of all, a beauty, with long blonde hair and long, shapely legs. Still, Pauline could not possibly have guessed that Martha would become the third Mrs. Ernest Hemingway.

Skinner, the three-hundred-pound black bartender at Sloppy Joe's, described Hemingway's first sighting of Martha as a meeting between "beauty and the beast." She was fetchingly attired in a black cotton sundress, he was sloppily dressed in a T-shirt and dirty Basque fishing shorts held up by a hemp rope. Ernest was delighted to meet a fellow novelist, particularly one who had read his books. They talked for hours.

Martha stayed on at the Colonial Hotel on Duval Street to work on a book. Soon she was invited to the Hemingway home. Said Miriam Williams, the cook: "There would be parties and Mr. Ernest and Miss Martha would be outside and kissing and carrying on, and I'd say to Miss Ada, 'Look at that, would you.' The way some people act."

Right after Martha left Key West, so did Ernest. In fact, they met in Miami and traveled together by train to New York. There he met with executives at the North American Newspaper Alliance and negotiated a contract for coverage of the Spanish Civil War. He was to be paid $500 for each cabled story and $1000 for longer pieces that were mailed. Soon after Hemingway reached Madrid Martha appeared, armed with a contract to cover the war for *Collier's* magazine, whose publisher Ernest had punched out in Bimini.

The affair with Martha marked the beginning of Hemingway's break with Pauline, with Key West and with the country of his birth. He began to spend less time on the island. The Thompsons were still friends but a coolness had arisen between them and Hemingway. Elsewhere around the town he met disapproving glances. He was no longer the Mahatma who could do no wrong.

Even the city was changing. The vision of Julius Stone and the hurricane of '35 had conspired to create a new Key West. Stone had set about converting a bankrupt fishing village into a tourist destination, building such attractions as the Key West Aquarium and providing more accommodations and amenities for visitors. After the hurricane destroyed the railroad tracks, the FEC sold its Keys bridges and right-of-way to the federal government. By 1938 the government had completed the Overseas Highway along the former railroad tracks.

U.S. 1 now extended all the way to the southeast tip of Key West. The island was finally accessible to lower-income tourists who drove down in the family car. Ernest was not comfortable with gawking sightseers.

When he wasn't in Spain, Hemingway was spending more and more time in Havana. He put on weight, fleshing out to 215, and his often-terrible temper was getting the best of him all too frequently. When he couldn't find the key to his workroom in the poolhouse, he seized a pistol and angrily shot the lock off. Pauline gave a party at the Havana Madrid night club on Front Street. Ernest spoiled it by getting into a fight, resulting in $187 in damages.

For a while Pauline rented an East 50th Street apartment in New York, near a private school where she had enrolled the boys. Ernest's visits to Havana became longer and more frequent. Martha leased an old estate near Havana for them, called La Finca Vigia, the "watch-tower." Here he continued to work on his novel of the Spanish Civil War. The manuscript had swollen to some 200,000 words.

Wright and Joan Langley

After the divorce a group which doesn't include Ernest gathers at the Hemingway home. Left to right are Lorine Thompson, Ester Anderson Chambers, Jane Mason, an unidentified man in back, Pauline, James "Sully" Sullivan, and Ginny Pfeiffer, Pauline's sister.

Martha went with him to his new U.S. hangout, Sun Valley, an Idaho ski resort. When she left in early November, 1939, to go back to work in Europe, Ernest was seized with a bout of loneliness. He decided he wanted to spend Christmas with his children and with Pauline in Key West.

On December 17 Ernest arrived at an empty house. No one was around except the gardener and his three children. Pauline had taken the boys and flown to New York for the holidays. Ernest stayed in the city for nine days, avoiding his old friends. He worked mornings and afternoons on *For Whom the Bell Tolls* and took his meals at downtown restaurants in a city that would not be his again until after his death.

He stayed in the empty house on Christmas Day—perhaps as a penance, James McLendon wrote. On December 26, 1939, he packed his bags, books and personal items in his Buick and boarded the ferry for Cuba. For the rest of his life he would live at La Finca Vigia in the village of San Francisco de Paula. For Ernest Miller Hemingway, aged 40, the toot of the Havana ferry whistle signaled farewell to Key West.

CHAPTER XI

◆ ◆ ◆ ◆ ◆ ◆ ◆ ◆ ◆ ◆ ◆

PAPA LIVES

IT WAS HEMINGWAY'S TOWN when he lived here. It's still his town. His impact today is so powerful it's hard to realize he is no longer around, walking at his jaunty pace down Duval Street, drinking a Scotch at Sloppy Joe's, tying up *Pilar* at the dock after a day of fishing in the Stream. Papa's face looks out at you from T-shirts bouncing along on the exciting anatomy of nubile young women or squeezed across the chests and pot-bellies of dedicated beer drinkers. A Margarita is lifted and the face of the man looks up at you from the drink's coaster. There are Hemingway caps and Hemingway sweatshirts. Hemingway's house, now a museum, is the island's No. 1 attraction, and the bar where he drank, Sloppy Joe's, is the most popular saloon in town. There is a Hemingway fishing tournament and a Hemingway Days Festival. There is even a Hemingway-Look-Alike Contest when Sloppy Joe's bulges with enough Papa clones to make you forget the Elvis sightings in Nashville or Las Vegas.

Hemingway left Key West at the end of December, 1939. He, of course, continued to visit his American home town for the rest of his life, usually for short stays. His old friends who had sided with Pauline in the divorce came back to him, though the friendships could never again be as close as they were in the days when a Key Wester's greatest honor was membership in the Mob.

On July 2, 1961, Ernest Hemingway killed himself in Ketchum, Idaho, shortly before his July 21st birthday. His birthday is the day that is commemorated in Key West with the annual Hemingway Days Festival. What is remembered is not the death but the bacchanalian joy of living of one of the twentieth century's greatest writers and one of its most entertaining legends.

HEMINGWAY DAYS

July in Key West. Hot. Steamy hot with the spell of a tropical sun baking the land below. But who cares? The streets by late afternoon are filled with noisy, happy throngs living it up in Margaritaville.

Hemingway Days Festival honors the July birthday of the patron saint of the island, Papa, the Great Mother of all Big Daddies. Thousands of revelers descend upon Key West for a week-long celebration. Hemingway the writer is celebrated the first part of the week, and Hemingway the zestful lover of life is celebrated during the second part when the weekend turns Key West into a mini-Mardi Gras.

Fittingly enough, the festival's birthplace was Sloppy Joe's, which was already tying Papa into its promotions. In 1981 Michael Whalton, manager of the saloon, read in the *Wall Street Journal* about a "bad Hemingway" contest in Los Angeles, a competition among parody writers. Why, he wondered, didn't Key West have an event to honor the man? Though not officially a Conch—he was born in Miami—Whalton has strong Key West ties. He is a descendant of an old island family, which includes a famous judge at the turn of the century, and can even point proudly to a Whalton Street, an honor Hemingway never attained. (Ironically, Key West does have a Pauline Street, though named for a much earlier Pauline than Ernest's second wife.) Michael pursued the idea with Ernest's brother, Leicester. The timing was perfect: the weekend closest to his July 21 birthday, a dead time in a city that depended on tourism.

The 1981 Hemingway Days Festival emerged as a three-day event a street fair, a running of the bulls, a short-story competition and a Hemingway Look-Alike contest. Leicester volunteered to judge the short stories, ably backed up by his daughter Hilary and by Lorian Hemingway, the author's granddaughter.

"We didn't know how many would show up for the Look-Alike contest," said Whalton. "I called everybody I knew who had a beard.

'Show up if you can,' I told them. We had about twelve or thirteen for the first night, about the same number the next night, then about seven or eight for the finals on Saturday night. Tom Feeney was a clear-cut winner."

The only failure in the first festival was the Running of the Bulls, a bizarre tribute to the famous dash in Pamplona, Spain, immortalized in *The Sun Also Rises.* In the Hemingway Days variation contestants did not attempt to outrun killer bulls but actually competed as bulls. Prizes were awarded to the best dressed and fastest bulls. "The run was only a block long but the temperature was ninety-two, too hot for a bull costume," said Whalton. The bull event was never repeated.

The following year the newly created Key West Tourist Development Council contributed funds and the festival began to blossom. That same year Leicester temporarily switched the dates of his Hemingway Billfish Tournament to beef up the festival. Most important of all, the Hemingway Home and Museum signed on as a sponsor. It became the site of the first "Characters in Costume" Party. Great souls stepped from the pages of his books and walked the house and grounds of his Key West mansion—Lady Brett Ashley and Jake Barnes, Santiago the old fisherman, Nick Adams, Pilar (the woman, not the boat), Harry Morgan and, oddly enough, a Portuguese Man-o'-War from the pages of *The Old Man and the Sea.*

From early on, the festival was staunchly supported by Ernest's extended family: his brother Les, until his death in 1982; Les's widow Doris and their daughters, screenwriter Hilary Hemingway Freundlich and Anne; Patrick's daughter Edwina (Mina); Gregory's son Edward and his novelist daughter Lorian, and Lorian's daughter, Cristen. Lorian, whose novel *Walking into the River*, was published in October, 1992, by Simon and Schuster, has coordinated the short-story contest from the start, ensuring Hemingway blood in maintaining high standards. Hilary remarked: "To us, Hemingway Days is a family reunion."

Within three years the festival had clearly established itself. Recalling the author's love of fisticuffs, Whalton added boxing exhibitions at a ring set up in the yard at Hemingway House. One year, two of Ernest's old sparring partners participated. Iron Baby Roberts refereed and Shine Forbes served as a judge. Songwriter Jimmy Buffett, who would later succumb to the Key West spell and become a novelist himself, volunteered to sing the National Anthem before the matches. When a commemorative Ernest Hemingway stamp was issued by the U.S. Postal Service, it was unveiled in Key West as part of the 1989 Hemingway Days Festival. The stamp featured the memorable 1957 photograph by Yousef Karsh, the same picture that adorns Sloppy Joe's T-shirts.

Hemingway Days Festival

A group of Hemingway Days revelers includes Look-Alike winners and Hemingway family members; back row, left to right: Bill Young, Hollywood, Florida; Leo Rost, Boynton Beach; Michael Dallett, Fort Lauderdale; and Nick Parrish, Pompano Beach; front row: Cristen Hemingway Jaynes, Ernest's great granddaughter; her mother, Lorian Hemingway; and Hilary Hemingway Freundlich, daughter of Leicester Hemingway.

By the mid-eighties, droves of beefy, bearded Papa clones were roaming Duval Street, looking for a drink to psych themselves up for the fierce competition. Some bring cheering sections, others print up posters and flyers to drum up support. The Look-Alike Contest has become far and away the most popular event of the festival—so popular in fact that even Oak Park, the sedate midwestern city where

Ernest was born, now holds one of its own. The Key West version attracts entrants from all over the country and from Europe; the 1991 winner was from Santa Fe. By 1992 the number of look-alikes had risen to eighty-three, one from as far away as Hawaii.

One of the entrants, Norman Levin from nearby Fort Lauderdale, brought a marital touch to the contest, perhaps an indirect tribute to Hemingway, who, like Levin, married four times. Norman had entered the contest every year since 1985 without winning; in 1992 he fell short again but this time he won something more important: the hand of his bride. The wedding invitation announced the nuptials of Norman "Papa" Levin and Paula "Pauline" Shapiro, of Baltimore. The wedding was held just prior to the contest. Music was nontraditional. As they marched down an aisle of look-alikes, a Frank Sinatra record delivered the strains of "Young at Heart." After the ceremony, exit music was the island anthem, Jimmy Buffett's immortal "Why Don't We Get Drunk and Screw." Only in Key West, as Papa would have said.

Like Levin, many of the contestants enter the contest year after year. George Burley, 57, of Tierra Verde, near St. Petersburg, Florida, won in 1992 after four unsuccessful tries. "Maybe it's because I'm older and the beard's a little grayer," he said. "I feel more like him than ever before."

The 1992 festival, which drew close to ten thousand people, included a wide variety of events, some of which would have delighted Papa and some of which would probably have infuriated him. After all, he did loathe tourism and its inevitable end-product—tourists. Key West radio featured a Hemingway trivia contest, and a story-telling contest was held at the Ocean Key House. Guided walking tours in the early evening acquainted visitors with the city's rich literary heritage for which Hemingway could claim considerable credit. On Friday night the Hemingway Home and Museum hosted a party, with music. For the athletic the festival offered backcountry kayak tours, a golf tournament, sailing races, the annual arm-wrestling contest and a 5K sunset run, which drew a winner from faraway Norway. Another contestant, Dave Meeker, was from Sacramento, California. His devotion to Hemingway runs so deep that his bookstore is named after the hero of many of the author's best short stories. He calls his store Nick Adams and Company, Rare Books.

As the fiesta developed, the founding fathers and mothers realized the festival had overemphasized one Hemingway at the expense of the other. During his highly public life he had emerged as two people, one a swaggering macho figure, the other a disciplined artist of rare genius. In the alcoholic haze of Hemingway Days, the writer had been shunted over to a table in the corner of a noisy barroom. The festival founders moved to correct the problem.

In 1987 Dr. James Plath, assistant professor of English at Illinois Wesleyan University, was visiting Key West to interview one of the island's most perceptive interpreters. The composer Jimmy Buffet, who had christened Key West "Margaritaville," would be the subject for a feature in *Clockwatch Review*, a "little" magazine which Plath edits and publishes. For the special edition he asked Lorian Hemingway, whose stories had appeared in such varied publications as *Rolling Stone*, *Penthouse* and *The New York Times Sunday Magazine*, to write an article on her great-uncle, Leicester Hemingway. She in turn asked him to serve as a judge for the short-story contest.

Hemingway Days Festival

Principals in the Hemingway Days Writers Workshop and Conference include author and Hemingway scholar Dr. James Nagel; screenwriter Hilary Hemingway Freundlich; Dr. James Plath, Workshop director; and novelist Lorian Hemingway.

From Plath's meetings with Lorian, Hilary Hemingway and her husband, writer Jeff Freundlich, and Michael Whalton emerged the Hemingway Days Writer's Workshop and Conference. "The impetus" she said, "was the success of the annual Key West Literary Seminar." The first workshop, held in 1989, drew just twelve registrants. By 1992 it had grown into a three-day session, featuring well-known writers including James Dickey, author of *Deliverance* and winner of the National Book Award for *Buckdancer's Choice.* Dickey was further honored with the first Conch Republic Prize for Literature. Others on the workshop staff were James W. Hall, author of three novels set in the Keys *Bones of Coral, Under Cover of Daylight* and *Tropical Freeze,* and James Nagel, professor of English at the University of Georgia, Hemingway scholar and author of *Hemingway in Love and War.*

"The idea of the workshops was to add a serious dimension to the festival," said Plath, who appeared at a Friday-night party at the Hemingway House clad in the Pamplona bull-runner's classic white togs accented with red sash. Less than two weeks earlier he had run with the bulls in Spain where he had presented a paper at the Fifth International Hemingway Conference. "We wanted to give people something of substance to take back."

Plath is attracted to Key West by many of the same elements that appealed to Hemingway. "The air is dense, rich, thick, strikes you in the face," he said. "Key West is a visual potpourri, plants fifty feet tall, tropical flora and fauna. Many of the elements that drew Hemingway are still in place, the sea, the fishing. And a dynamic, robust life style. That's the Key West personality."

Plath, who has written on the relationship between modern art and the work of Hemingway, compares the author in one sense to the famous Spanish surrealist Salvador Dali: "They were the first successful self-promoters in their respective art forms."

That sense of self-promotion played a major role in creating the author's 1990s image. Said Plath: "Hemingway was raised on romantic legends. He understood their power. Now Hemingway cults have grown up. He's been set up as a guru, a figure who represents escapism, romance. He's also a symbol of what people would like to do with their lives. Today it's the Hemingway legend that is celebrated as much as the Nobel laureate's work."

At the Key West Island Bookstore on Fleming Street sales of Hemingway books pick up sharply at festival time. John Boisnault, who collected and studied Hemingwayana even before he bought the store in 1986, said: "Hemingway is our biggest selling author, about fifteen per cent of our volume on new, used and rare books. The most popular book is his Key West book, *To Have and Have Not,* followed by *The Old Man and the Sea,* and then three more books that sell about equally, *A Farewell to Arms, The Sun Also Rises* and *For Whom the Bell Tolls.*" Preferences for Hemingway books follow the same pattern at the book shop at the Hemingway House Museum.

Key West's biggest Hemingway literary event was the third annual Key West Literary Seminar, held in January, 1985, at the Tennessee Williams Fine Arts Center. The entire three-day program was devoted to Papa. Digby Diehl, book editor of the *Los Angeles Examiner,* summed it up well: "During three days of intensive study, experts described how Hemingway fished for marlin, drank rum, sparred with his pals, and wrote six of his greatest works here. And his spirit is still alive in the old haunts, they implied. You need only the courage—and the liver—to search, bar after bar, for Papa."

Among the Hemingway authorities who spoke at the seminar were George Plimpton, founder and editor of the *Paris Review;* Charles Scribner, Jr., representing Hemingway's publisher; Papa's son, Patrick, returning to his childhood home for the first time in nearly 35 years, and a number of Hemingway scholars and authors, among them Bernice Kert, Robert Gajdusek, James Nagel, Scott Donaldson, Donald Junkins, David Kaufelt, Linda Wagner-Martin, Paul Smith, Allen Josephs, Frank Laurance, Michael Reynolds and Tim O'Brien.

Playwright John de Groot's one-man play, *Papa,* had its world premiere as a workshop performance at the Hemingway literary festival. He calls his play "a one-man docu-drama; a theatrical encounter with a 19th-century Ulysses lost in the 20th century." Hemingway gravitated to the island because, says de Groot, "Key West was a 19th century environment." The playwright told Rosemary

Jones, who was writing a story for *Gold Coast* magazine: "All the things that Hemingway did were almost caricatures of a 19th-century archetypal American patriarch. The great white hunter. It's Kiplingesque, it's like Teddy Roosevelt. He was a bully man. He did things with manly vigor. He was a warrior." The July pilgrimage, de Groot believes, is peopled by men who come to Key West looking for a father image, looking for the patriarchal archetype, a role played with rare skill by Papa. Said de Groot: "A ball-scratching, hard-drinking woman chaser, this was his image. And Key West bought it."

Papa the Legend has a greater impact on Key West today than Hemingway the Writer had when he lived here. He was the town's celebrity then but the glow faded after he moved to Cuba. Joan Langley, a Conch who now operates the publishing company Langley Press, Inc., with her husband Wright, recalls growing up in Key West: "In high school we read Tennessee Williams, not Hemingway. I never read him until I went away to Duke. Our neighbor was Charles Thompson and my father worked for Norberg Thompson. I never dreamed that Mr. Sullivan, a very nice old man, had been a drinking buddy of Hemingway's. He used to repair my tricycle. We used to hear stories that Hemingway's mob would go to Sully's machine shop to sniff oxygen to cure their hangovers."

Wright Langley, author of three books on the Keys, one in collaboration with Joan, calls Hemingway "a fairly recent phenomenon." Langley is a historical consultant, specializing in Key West and the Florida Keys following fifteen years as manager of the Historical Florida Keys Preservation Board. Langley Press published a 1990 edition of *Papa*, James McLendon's book on Hemingway's Key West years. A native of North Carolina, Langley arrived in Key West in 1965 to work as a reporter for the *Miami Herald*'s Keys Bureau.

"In 1965 not that much attention was paid to Hemingway. You might drop by Hemingway's bar, Sloppy Joe's, in late afternoon and find maybe ten people in there." Tourism began to bloom, he believes, after the 1976 Bicentennial, when a strong program of restoration coupled with more promotion began the upswing.

Meanwhile, both the Hemingway Home and Museum and

Sloppy Joe's had increased their promotion, thus setting the stage for Hemingway Days and the formation of the Tourist Development Commission in the early 1980s.

Most active in exploiting Hemingway has been Sloppy Joe's. The heavy promotion began in the late 1970s when Stan Smith began selling T-shirts, featuring the famous Karsh photograph of the author in his later years. Sightings of these shirts have been reported in Europe, Africa and Australia. Sloppy Joe's sells some one hundred thousand of these shirts a year, says manager John Klausing. The saloon also sells Hemingway polo shirts, muscle shirts, sweat shirts, ponchos, caps and straw hats, coasters, mugs, shot glasses, pens and postcards. For $4.25 the saloon sells one of Hemingway's favorite drinks, the Papa Dobles, a Daiquiri variation, which uses the juice of a ruby red grapefruit, cherry juice and rum.

Media coverage has been steady for both the Hemingway Home and Sloppy Joe's. On a November morning Klausing was interviewed for the syndicated television show "A Current Affair" one day after

Photo by Stuart McIver

Key West's 1990s *Pilar*, a charterboat and floating Hemingway Museum.

being invaded by group of eleven Dutch reporters.

Sloppy Joe's functions also as a Hemingway museum. Its walls are covered with photographs of the man and his world-wide activities. Erik Smith's 1933 WPA-period painting showing Hemingway at work still hangs in the bar, as does a contemporary painting of Sloppy Joe's by Carol Sadowski, of Hollywood, Florida. Actually the town is home to three Hemingway museums: the Hemingway House, the largest and most popular; Sloppy Joe's, where the drinks rank somewhat higher than the memorabilia; and a small one aboard Tex Phillips' *Pilar II.* Built in the 1930s to roughly the same specifications as Papa's boat, the Phillips craft houses a collection of photographs, a watercolor and movie posters from films made from Hemingway's books.

Novelist David Kaufelt, who conducts walking tours of the island's literary sites, wrote in *The Book Lover's Guide to Florida*: "Hemingway, America's first great literary media celebrity, an early master of publicity spin, came via Cuba from Europe in 1928 on the recommendation of his friend, John Dos Passos, who had visited during a walking tour. Hemingway arrived at the beginning of his fame and the onset of his personal myth. His life in Key West was well chronicled in Pathé newsreels and *Life* magazine, helping to create an image of Key West as a writers' haven."

Long after he left Key West for Cuba, the Hemingway aura continued to pull novelists, playwrights, poets, biographers, historians, editors and publishers into his magnetic field. In *Key West Writers and Their Houses* Lynn Mitsuko Kaufelt, David's wife, wrote: "But I believe the reason so many writers thrive in Key West is that the houses they write in and the houses around them are filled with the traditions and the histories and the life that helped spark that illusive creative fire."

The Key West literary colony has included such writers as poets Elizabeth Bishop, Richard Wilbur, James Merrill and John Malcolm Brinnin; novelists Phil Caputo, Robert Stone, Thomas Sanchez and Thomas McGuane; and America's premier playwright, Tennessee Williams.

"I feel that Hemingway's spirit remains in the sea, contained in a fabled big marlin forever circling our island, threatening and challenging and ultimately encouraging those following in his wake," explained David Kaufelt. "Key West suddenly became this literary place, mostly because of Hemingway."

Painters feel the pull of Papa too. Artist Carol Sadowski, compared by one art critic with the American painter Edward Hopper, visited the Hemingway house for the first time in 1977. Since then she has gone on to paint nearly forty pictures interpreting Hemingway themes, starting with Key West and then branching out to his other locales: Oak Park, where he was born, Paris, Spain, Bimini and Cuba.

Obviously a presence as mighty as Ernest Hemingway's does not go quietly into the tropical night. Traces of his Key West days mingle everywhere with commercial tie-ins. Even pizza.

Authors and scholars search the town, looking for Hemingway the Writer. Others inhale his legend through a tour of his house, a day in the Gulf Stream stalking the mighty marlin, or a night of pub-crawling in the saloons of Key West.

It really doesn't matter where you go. He's still here.

LOOK-ALIKES

Hemingways to the right of me. Hemingways to the left of me. Too many Hemingways. Eighty-three altogether—and I was one of those Papa clones, packed like olives in the sweltering heat of Sloppy Joe's.

Each July Key West lures tourists to the Conch Republic with its annual Hemingway Days Festival, timed to honor the birthday of the city's favorite son. The most popular event: the Hemingway Look-Alike Contest.

Thirty-five of us Papas were clustered around the stage, gazing out at a sweating, beer- and/or tequila-guzzling multitude that had overwhelmed Hemimgway's favorite saloon. Overhead, paddle fans swirled the hot, beery vapors and the deafening sounds of a country rock band.

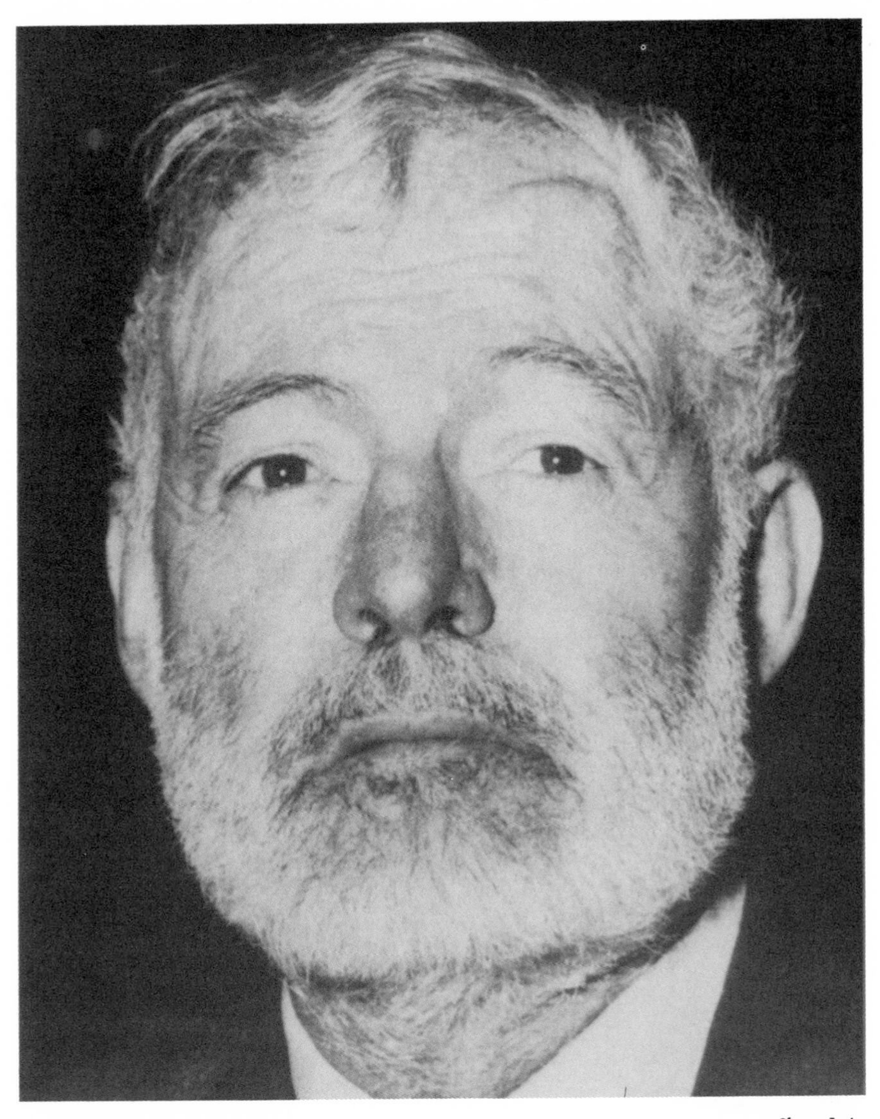

Sloppy Joe's

The Look-Alike contest aims at the appearance of the Great Man sported in the late 1950s, as in this 1959 photograph, taken in Pamplona, Spain.

Any minute now I would be going out on the stage to do my best to look, swagger and sound like the Great Man. In my head I rehearsed my lines again and waited. And waited.

Ruth Chados, contest coordinator, told me: "Keep it short. Tell them it's time to party. They've been drinking for hours and they're in no mood to hear a speech."

On the drive down I had rehearsed my lines. I would dazzle the crowd and the judges—former winners and members of the Hemingway family—with a great Hemingway quote, backed up with an impressive stage prop. I would swagger out with a half-empty bottle of champagne in my hand. And in spell-binding fashion I would deliver one of my favorite Hemingway quotes:

"The half empty champagne bottle is the enemy of mankind."

I would move then to Phase 2, the literary element, a high-toned touch I was sure no one else would duplicate. I would deliver the earth-shaking announcement that I was writing a book on Papa. This had to be a winner with judges and crowd.

"We seek the older, heavier set Hemingway look-alike, with the full beard. Judging is based on the personal appearance," read the guidelines." Hefty, burly, bearded. I decided to wear khaki shorts and a khaki shirt, enhanced by a touch of Hemingway realism. Papa often held his khaki shorts up not by a belt but by a piece of rope that sometimes smelled of dead fish. I skipped the dead fish touch.

I donned my khaki outfit, tied a rope around my middle, combed my hair and beard, then sprayed them with hair glue.

Why did I think I might win this contest? I wasn't nearly hefty enough. I'm just six feet tall and weigh about 180. He was six two and weighed about 220, sometimes even more. His face was round, mine long and thin.

But then I had a secret weapon. I looked like other people. Something about my face tapped into a giant Everyman motherlode. Most of my look-alike experiences were harmless, but a couple bordered on dangerous.

Years ago, for example, as a young sportswriter for a North Carolina daily, I covered a fight between a local favorite, Mickey

Whelan, and a visiting welterweight, one Irish Johnny Taylor. The fight ended early. Irish Johnny hit Mickey below the belt and Mickey couldn't go on. Fight fans were not happy. After the fight the crowd mistook me for Irish Johnny. I had to run to get away from a howling mob.

Then in Washington, at Ebbitt's Old Ale House, a historic saloon which claimed Abe Lincoln as a satisfied customer, a mean-looking character with an eye twitch said to me: "You think we aren't on to you. You FBI people think you can get away with anything. You haven't got anything on us and you're not going to." His eye kept twitching and I felt like mine would start up soon. I left.

My Uncle Bob was a friend of the family of the great North Carolina novelist Thomas Wolfe, a contemporary of Hemingway's. One night he took me to one of the Washington suburbs to visit Wolfe's sister, Mabel, better known as Helen Gant in Wolfe's most famous novel, *Look Homeward Angel.* As we sat on her front porch one summer night, she said: "Mr. McIver, how strange. The way the light hits you you look like Tom."

Another time I got on an elevator in a Baltimore hotel with a powerful U.S. Senator, Millard Tydings. "Young man," he said, "You remind me of an actor I used to know, Frank Craven." I was flattered. Craven had starred in Thornton Wilder's *Our Town* on Broadway, not to mention assorted movies.

You can see why I thought I might have a shot at winning the Hemingway contest. All I needed was a judging panel of Senator Tydings, Mabel Wolfe Wheaton and an angry mob of fight fans.

When I got to Sloppy Joe's, I told Ruth Chados: "I've got two speeches, one thirty seconds, one sixty seconds."

She stared at me in wonderment. "You've got about twenty seconds; fifteen would be better. These people have been drinking for hours. They have no attention span."

Mike Whalton, festival director announced the prizes—among them a week for two at the Ocean Key House, a $100 bar tab at Sloppy Joe's, and "last of all, an oil change at Boa's Tire and Auto Service." The oil change got a laugh.

Next he began to call up Hemingways in groups of five. I watched with dismay. All were burlier than I was and clearly rounder of face. And their messages to the throng were all brief, mostly calls to the faithful to drink up. Some clones had their own cheering sections. Many had competed in the contest for years. One, the aptly-named George Burley, said it was his fifth try.

I stood just off stage, my half-empty champagne bottle resting on the table of a happy band of revelers. Then I heard my name called. I just left the champagne bottle there. Later some waitress would pick it up and be completely mystified. A half-empty champagne bottle in a beer and tequila room. And to make it even more mysterious the bottle was in a J.C. Penney bag.

Photo by Peter Colelli

The author with a beard grown for the Hemingway Look-Alike Contest.

Waves of heat and room noise buffeted me. I tried to swagger as I said:

"One true sentence, as Hemingway would put it." I felt a brief wave of disapproval. Was I going to be one of those talkers? I went on with the true sentence: "The best place in the world to be today is Sloppy Joe's." Mild approval. I decided to take a chance. "One more true sentence. My car does need an oil change."

Finally, a ripple of subdued laughter. The only laugher to gladden my heart was that of Hilary Hemingway Freundlich, Ernest's niece. Who just happened to be one of the judges. Maybe I might get Hilary's vote.

Thirty-five Hemingways were trotted up on stage that night. Nine qualified for the Saturday night finals. Somehow my name didn't get called. Five months later I met Lorian Hemingway, Ernest's granddaughter. She advised: "If you're going to enter the contest again, gain some weight, a lot of weight."

In the Saturday night finals George Burley won on his fifth try and I was left to ponder why I didn't win. The main reason, I think, was that there were at least a dozen people there who looked more like Hemingway than I did. Heftier, rounder of face, earthier.

But there was something else. I think I impersonated the wrong Hemingway. Two Hemingways left their mark on this world, one a dedicated, disciplined writer, winner of the Nobel Prize, one of the two or three most important writers of the twentieth century.

The other was a self-promoting celebrity who projected to the world the image of Papa, a man who could shoot more big game, catch bigger sailfish, get into more fights, chase more women and drink more booze than anybody else on the planet. That Hemingway was the quintessential Party Animal, the patron saint of Key West.

This is the Hemingway that is honored at Sloppy Joe's every July, a lover of life, joyful and exuberant. The men all wanted to be like him, the women all wanted to spend the night with him.

Party on, Papa.

CONCH REPUBLIC

In the spring of 1982 the Reagan Administration set up a roadblock just south of Florida City on U.S. 1, the only road to Key West. On a Sunday afternoon the United States Border Patrol began stopping all cars coming back to the mainland from the Keys. Weary, sunburned tourists were checked for illegal drugs and aliens. Traffic backed up for twenty-three miles. Tempers and bladders backed up for at least as far.

Irate motorists protested, and attorneys challenged the clumsy, ineffective blockade in the courts. The Conchs, of course, were livid. The Keys depended on tourism and the government was harassing credit-card-carrying, money-spending tourists. There was only one answer. War.

The idea for the Conch Republic was born on April 20, 1982. Key West Mayor Dennis Wardlow and five other revolutionaries, Dennis Bitner, William E. Smith, Edwin O. Swift, III, Townsend Keiffer and John Magiola, met to plot a counterstrike. Three days later the six "Conch Reveres" called a town meeting at noon in Mallory Square, named after a Key West Confederate hero who had seceded more than a century earlier.

Their call that April day was for Key West to secede from the Union, form the Conch Republic and declare war on the tyrant. A Conch Republic flag was raised on high. Impassioned speeches were made, a few ambassadorships were passed out and a loaf of stale Cuban bread was tossed aloft to symbolize, somewhat murkily, a declaration of war against the United States.

Then, suddenly, the Conch Republic surrendered and applied for foreign aid. The aid was fast in coming. The roadblock was lifted.

The party lasted a week. Since then Conch Republic Days has become an annual event. Border passes and passports are printed and silver coins, T-shirts and flags are sold. The Conch Republic, born from an assault on tourism, quickly became another sterling idea for promoting Key West tourism. Mayor Wardlow continues as prime minister.

The Hemingway boys—Ernest and Les—got there first with the idea even though Ernest was dead set against tourists taking over his island. Still, here's what he said in a revolutionary letter written to John Dos Passos from Key West on April 12, 1932, almost exactly fifty years before the Conch Republic was born. He called for the establishment of the South Western Island Republic. He proposed that Key West secede from the Union immediately, the day after the Navy and Marines began to deactivate the naval base. He wrote:

"I have organized cutting the cables, blowing up Bahia Honda viaduct, burning bridges, destroying all buoys and lighthouses and the seizing of enough tramp steamers to feed the ungry (sic) populace. We will be a free port, set up gigantic liquor warehouses and be most PROSPEROUS ISLAND IN THE WORLD. The PARIS OF THE SOUTH WEST."

Hemingway had some bloody plans and an approach guaranteed to offend everybody. Decidedly not "politically correct." He planned to re-enslave the blacks and use the car ferries to Cuba to run "chinamen." His old friend, Sully Sullivan, was to be put to work building a guillotine, for considerable carnage lay ahead.

"On the first night we massacre the catholics and the jews," he proposed, an odd directive since he, his wife and his two sons were Catholics. "The second the protestants who have been lulled into a false sense of security by the events of the first evening. The third night we butcher the free thinkers, atheists, communists and members of the lighthouse service. The fourth day we fish the gulf and capture another ship to feed our faithful jigs. That evening we knock off a few counter revolutionaries and if things aren't going well we burn the town. The fifth and sixth days are free and members of the party can amuse themselves as they like. On the Seventh day we elect Butstein (Dos Passos' wife Katy) the Goddess of Reason and order MacLeish to write an Epic Poem about the Movement. Late that evening we shoot MacLeish as his poem has turned out Lousy and send for Evan Shipman [another poet friend of Hemingway's]. You can see how it will be. Just one gay hilarious round with everyone busy and happy. At the end of twelve days we raise wages to beat hell and massacre the poles."

Ernest's younger brother, the hefty Leicester, had a plan that was much more elaborate and not at all bloody. His republic was not located at Key West. New Atlantis, as he called his island nation, was a raft anchored off the south coast of Jamaica in the early 1960s.

Lorian Hemingway, Ernest's granddaughter, wrote a funny account of New Atlantis in *The Clockwatch Review* in 1986: "The flag for New Atlantis was stitched by Les' wife, Doris. It was made of dark blue cloth, with a white interior triangle representing the Bermuda Triangle. The white piece of cloth was salvaged from one of Hilary's diapers. Les and a friend took a hollowed-out log canoe to the site of New Atlantis, which had been raised on a sea mount, to raise the new country's flag. Les hoped to receive mail on the raft in time. He processed stamps for the new country, and minted coins. He was president then of a country wrought from idealism and a sense of humor. The Constitution of New Atlantis was modeled after that of the United States...The truth is that Les Hemingway could have stood in shallow water and proclaimed himself an island and republic unto himself."

CHAPTER XII

◆ ◆ ◆ ◆ ◆ ◆ ◆ ◆ ◆ ◆ ◆

WALK WITH PAPA

EVERWHERE YOU GO on the island his face looks out at you, mostly from T-shirts, sometimes from coasters underneath a drink, sometimes from posters advertising Hemingway Days or literary seminars. Burly men who may never have read any of his books or stories grow beards in the heat of a Key West July to compete in Hemingway look-alike contests.

No doubt about it, Ernest "Papa" Hemingway is the favorite son of Key West—the symbol, the human logo of the exotic, hedonistic island that lies at the tip of the Florida Keys, an island he called "the St. Tropez of the poor."

Here for over a decade he lived, fathered children, made friends and enemies, ate, drank, fished, fought, created his macho image, chased after women, worshipped, ripped his second marriage apart and somewhere along the way found time to write all or part of five fiction and nonfiction books, a play, *The Fifth Column*, and two of his most famous short stories, "The Snows of Kilimanjaro" and "The Short Happy Life of Francis Macomber."

The Great Man left his stamp on Key West. It was his town then. It's his town now. Let's trace a few of his large footsteps with a self-guided tour of Hemingway's hangouts, most of them in the northwestern part of the island, an area called Old Town. The starting place has to be his home at 907 Whitehead Street; his presence remains strong here, and the guided tour introduces the walker to the man. Allowing forty-five minutes for the tour of his home, the walk, which is roughly two miles long, should take you between an hour and a half and two hours.

HEMINGWAY HOUSE

After the many cold winters he spent in tiny Paris apartments, the spacious, lushly landscaped Spanish Colonial mansion built in 1851 of coral rock brought Hemingway under the spell of the tropics. In December of 1931 Ernest and his second wife, Pauline Pfeiffer, moved into their new home, a wedding present from Pauline's wealthy uncle, Gus Pfeiffer. It cost him just $8,000 then.

Historical Association of Southern Florida

The Hemingway House, the start of the Hemingway Walking Tour.

A restless expatriate who lived most of his adult life outside his native land, Hemingway seemed most at home in his own country in Depression-era Key West. Certainly, it was in this house that he worked best.

Seated in a Cuban cigarmaker's wooden chair, the author went to work early and wrote in longhand in an open room uncluttered with furniture on the second floor of the former carriage house. A good morning's work, he said, was "seven pencils." Bookshelves and trophies from his big game hunting expeditions adorn the walls. The

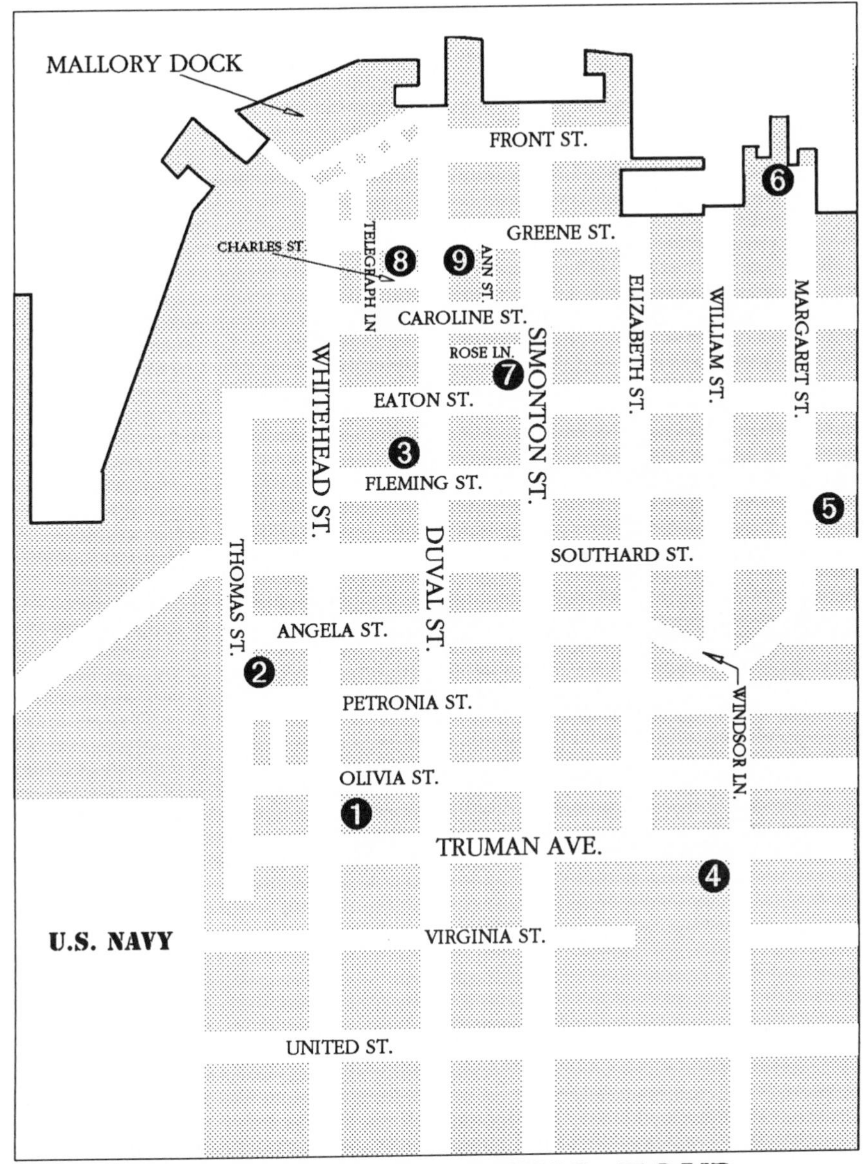

HEMINGWAY WALKING TOUR

1. Hemingway House
2. Boxing Arena
3. Colonial Hotel
4. St. Mary
5. Electric Kitchen
6. Thompson's Docks
7. First Apartment
8. First Sloppy Joe's
9. Second Sloppy Joe's

first room remodeled after the Hemingways moved in, the studio was entered via a second-story catwalk from the house. Today visitors on guided tours of the house climb outside stairs to see where the author worked.

While Ernest was in Spain in 1937, Pauline had a swimming pool built as a surprise for her roving husband. The first ever built in Key West, it cost $20,000, two-and-a-half times the purchase price of the house.

His reaction was unexpected. Reaching into his pocket, he pulled out a penny and threw it to the ground, angrily accusing Pauline of spending his last cent on the pool. Actually, it was her money. She took it all in good humor. She retrieved the penny and had it cemented into the ground with a glass covering. Visitors get a good laugh at Papa's last penny.

The grounds swarm with beautiful, six-toed cats, which found their way to Hemingway's after their owner died. One legend has it that Ernest acquired a urinal from Sloppy Joe's, put it on his back and carried it home to serve as a watering trough for the cats that hung around his home.

After Hemingway's death in 1961, the house was sold to Mrs. Bernice Dickson. It was designated a Registered National Historic Landmark in 1968. The Hemingway House is open every day from 9:00 A.M. to 5:00 P.M. for guided tours. Admission is $6.00 for adults, $1.50 for children. A gift shop sells T-shirts, note cards, pictures and books by and about Hemingway.

After seeing the house, walk north on Whitehead, turn left at Petronia Street, then proceed for two blocks to the northeast corner of the intersection of Petronia and Thomas streets.

FISTICUFFS

Now the Blue Heaven Restaurant, in Hemingway's day this site was an open-air boxing arena where he refereed the popular Friday night fights. Many of the fighters, among them "Iron Baby" Roberts, Kermit "the Battling Geech" Forbes and Alfred "Black Pie" Colebrooks, also boxed with Ernest in a ring in his backyard. They were paid fifty cents a round.

Photo by Stuart McIver

Where fists once flew the Blue Heaven Pool Room and Restaurant now operate.

From the Blue Heaven Restaurant walk back east on Petronia to Duval Street, then turn left to the northwest corner of Duval and Fleming.

COLONIAL HOTEL

In April, 1928, Ernest and Pauline Hemingway visited the city for the first time, sailing into Key West from Havana aboard a Peninsular & Occidental steamship. As they approached the island, the first sight they saw was the town's tallest building, the seven-story Key West Colonial Hotel. Later they would book visiting friends and relatives into the Colonial. Rates were reasonable: $1 to $6 a day, depending on whether you picked the American or the European Plan. The hotel is still in business today as the Holiday Inn-La Concha Resort.

From La Concha, walk east on Fleming Street. At 513 Fleming you will find the Key West Island Bookstore, well stocked with books by and about Papa Hemingway. In Hemingway's time the city's principal bookstore, owned by Leonte Valladares, was located at 517 Fleming. L. Valladares & Son is now at 1200 Duval Street, also well stocked with Hemingway books.

Photo by Joan McIver

The Holiday Inn - La Concha Resort does business today in the "skyscraper" that gave Hemingway his first glimpse of downtown Key West.

Proceed to Elizabeth Street, on past the Monroe County Public Library, filled with Hemingway material, to William Street. Next turn right to Windsor Lane, then turn left to the Key West Cemetery, where Windsor jogs right. Continue past Poorhouse Lane to Truman Avenue. Watch out for a killer cactus which sometimes attacks pedestrians in Windsor's 700 block.

ST. MARY, STAR OF THE SEA

A Congregationalist in his earlier years, Hemingway converted to Catholicism when he married the devoutly Catholic Pauline. He attended Mass at St. Mary, Star of the Sea, located at the southeast corner of Truman Avenue and Windsor Lane. Hemingway was generous to the church, recalls Betty Bruce, whose late husband, Toby, worked for Hemingway. "Ernest gave an altar to the church," she recalls.

Photo by Joan McIver

Ernest attended Mass at St. Mary, Star of the Sea.

From St. Mary, retrace your steps on Windsor Lane to the Key West Cemetery. There are no Hemingway associations here, except the graves of a few of his friends, but you might want to look at the monument to the sailors killed in the explosion of the USS Maine in 1898 or, if you can find it, the headstone which proclaims, "I Told You I Was Sick."

At the cemetery turn right on Passover Lane, then turn left on Margaret Street to the southeast corner of Margaret and Fleming Streets. Through this part of town you are seeing the old Key West that Hemingway knew.

ELECTRIC KITCHEN

At 830 Fleming Street Mrs. Rhoda Baker, better known as "Rutabaga," operated Mrs. Baker's Electric Kitchen. Despite the high-tech name, it was generally agreed that the only thing electric about the place was its lighting, supplied rather mundanely by a few bare light bulbs hanging from the ceiling. No matter. The food was good, plentiful and cheap. In 1935 the Electric Kitchen offered "club breakfast, 20 cents to 45 cents, luncheon and dinner, 30 to 50 cents." Mrs. Baker's place became a favorite hangout for Hemingway's "Mob," a strange combination of local pals and out-of-town talent.

From the Electric Kitchen continue north on Margaret Street to the waterfront area now known as Land's End Village.

Photo by Stuart Mciver

You can no longer get a twenty-cent breakfast at 830 Fleming Street, former home of the Electric Kitchen.

THOMPSON'S DOCKS

On Key West Bight Hemingway often visited docks owned by his closest friend, Charles Thompson. The three Thompson brothers, comprising the most affluent family on the island, owned a ship's chandlery, an icehouse, a cigarbox factory, a hardware and tackle store, a green turtle cannery and large waterfront pens called the Turtle Kraals. At one time the Thompsons controlled the green sea turtle industry in the Florida Keys and in Central America. The site of their turtle cannery is known today as Turtle Kraals, a restaurant, bar and museum.

Photo by Stuart McIver

Thompson's Docks would later become the Land's End Village.

When he first came to Key West, Ernest, an enthusiastic fisherman since his boyhood days, had to fish from charter boats or from the boats of his favorite Key West fishing buddies, Thompson, Sloppy Joe Russell and Captain Bra Saunders, a Bahamian. In 1934 Hemingway had a 38-foot powerboat custom built for him at the Wheeler Shipyard, City Island, New York. He would name his boat *Pilar*. He berthed his boat not at Thompson's Docks but in the Navy Yard, near the submarine pens, an area not open to the public. *Pilar* is now at Cojimar, Cuba.

From Land's End go south one block to Caroline, then walk west to the southwest corner of Caroline and Simonton Streets.

FIRST HOME

At 314 Simonton Street stands Casa Antigua, now a large private home with shops on the first floor. Through a bizarre sequence of events it turned out to be the first Key West domicile for the Hemingways.

Photo by Joan McIver

Casa Antigua, where the Hemingways stayed on their first visit to Key West, now contains shops on its first floor, among them the Pelican Poop Shoppe.

Pauline's uncle, Gus Pfeiffer, the principal owner of Richard Hudnut Pharmaceuticals, gave his favorite niece and her husband a superb wedding present, a yellow Model A Ford runabout. It was supposed to be waiting for them when they steamed into Key West from Havana. Unfortunately, problems with the ferry service from Miami to Key West had delayed the shipment of their new automobile.

Unable to find the car at the docks, Ernest called the local Ford dealership, the Trevor and Morris Company. Mortified that his car had not yet arrived, the dealers insisted that the Hemingways move into the Trevor and Morris Apartments while the problem was being worked out. The apartment, a drab set of rooms above the garage, was hardly first-rate. Its fame rests solely on its status as Ernest Hemingway's first Key West home. He immediately resumed work on *A Farewell to Arms.*

Now turn north to Greene Street and walk west past Duval.

THE BLIND PIG

With the end of Prohibition in 1933, Hemingway's pal, Josie Russell, charterboat captain and rumrunner, leased a dark cavernous speakeasy at 428 Greene Street. His plan was to convert it into a legal bar. Hemingway, who somewhere along the way became Russell's silent partner, convinced Josie that "Sloppy Joe's" would be a better name for the bar than the one it already sported—the Blind Pig.

Since there were no closing hours in Key West, Sloppy Joe's had no doors. A rowdy fisherman's bar, it quickly became Hemingway's favorite hangout. There he met Martha Gellhorn, author and foreign correspondent, stylishly clad in a black dress and sporting an impressive mane of tawny blonde hair and a shapely pair of legs. She later became his third wife.

On May 5, 1937, Josie Russell moved Sloppy Joe's half a block to the east. The bar where Ernest met Martha continued as a Key West institution under the name Captain Tony's. Follow Sloppy Joe's move

Photo by Joan McIver

Known once as the Blind Pig, then Sloppy Joe's, this Greene Street institution now goes by the name of Captain Tony's.

by walking east on Greene Street to the southeast corner of Greene and Duval.

SLOPPY JOE'S

When the Hemingways first arrived in Key West, the building at the southeast corner of Duval and Greene Streets housed the finest restaurant in town, the Victoria. It was owned and operated by a Spaniard with the embarrassing name of Farto.

It became Sloppy Joe's because the rent at 428 Greene Street had been raised a dollar a week. Rather than pay the increased rent, Joe Russell bought the Victoria for $2500 and moved in promptly in May of 1937.

Along with the Hemingway House, Sloppy Joe's remains to this day the Key West landmark most closely identified with the literary giant not with his literature but with his drinking and carousing. But in the last years of the 1930s Papa would spend less time in Key West. His second marriage was coming apart and his work was taking him often to Spain and Cuba. In 1940 he divorced Pauline and promptly married Martha Gellhorn. For most of the rest of his life his home would be the town of San Francisco de Paula, near Havana, Cuba.

Since his death by his own hand in 1961, Hemingway has

Photo by Joan McIver

Hemingway aficionados made a point of hoisting a cold one at Sloppy Joe's.

become more popular than ever in Key West. Some estimates claim that a million tourists a year come into the bar for a drink or just to have a peek at the Hemingway memorabilia. Newspaper clippings adorn the walls, along with paintings both by the WPA-period artist Erik Smith, whose oil shows Papa, Josie and the giant bartender, Skinner, and by the contemporary Hollywood, Florida, painter Carol Sadowski, who has depicted Sloppy Joe's in the early 1980s. Sales of Sloppy Joe's T-shirts, featuring a likeness of Hemingway, exceed a hundred thousand a year. They are now seen around the world. Although beer is still popular, today's patrons also drink vodka, tequila and various sweet frozen drinks. The Papa Dobles, the drink created to honor the author, sells now for $4.25.

A SIDE TRIP

The Casa Marina, the island's luxury hotel in Hemingway's time, is too far from other sites to fit into the walking tour. You might, however, want to drive to the hotel at 1500 Reynolds Street on the Atlantic Ocean. It was built in 1921 by the Flagler System, the same organization that brought the railroad to Key West nine years earlier. Hemingway used to eat at the Casa Marina on occasion, usually when visiting friends or

Photo by Joan McIver

In Hemingway's day the Casa Marina was the island's ritziest hotel.

business acquaintances invited him over. The management was not happy with his disdain for their dining dress code, particularly the absence of socks on his sandaled feet. He did, however, yield slightly by wearing long trousers, hopefully with a leather belt instead of a rope. The hotel today is known as Marriott's Casa Marina.

A HEMINGWAY CHRONOLOGY

July 21, 1899– Ernest Miller Hemingway born in Oak Park, Illinois.
July 8, 1918– Ernest wounded while serving in Italy as World War I ambulance driver.
Sept. 3, 1921–Ernest marries Hadley Richardson in Horton Bay, Michigan.
1926–*The Sun Also Rises* published.
May 10, 1927–EH marries Pauline Pfeiffer in Paris.
April, 1928–EH arrives in Key West.
Sept. 27, 1929–*A Farewell to Arms* published.
April 29, 1931–Hemingways acquire home on Whitehead Street.
1932–*Death in the Afternoon* published.
1933– *Winner Take Nothing* published.
May, 1934–*Pilar* arrives in Key West.
1935-*Green Hills of Africa* published.
1936–Two major stories published, "The Snows of Kilimanjaro" in *Esquire* and "The Short Happy Life of Francis Macomber" in *Cosmopolitan.*
December, 1936–Martha Gellhorn meets EH in Sloppy Joe's on Greene Street.
Oct. 15, 1937–Hemingway's Key West novel *To Have and Have Not,* published.
1938–*The Fifth Column and the First Forty-Nine Stories* published.
Dec. 26, 1939–Hemingway moves from Key West to San Francisco de Paula, Cuba.
1940–*For Whom the Bell Tolls* published.
Nov. 21. 1940–EH marries Martha Gellhorn, Cheyenne, Wyoming.
March 14, 1946–Hemingway weds Mary Welsh, Cuba.
1952–*The Old Man and the Sea* published.
1953–EH awarded Pulitzer Prize for *Old Man.*
1954–Hemingway awarded Nobel Prize for Literature.
July 2, 1961–Ernest Hemingway kills himself in Ketchum, Idaho.

BIBLIOGRAPHY

Anon. *A Guide to Key West.* New York: Hastings House, 1941.

Baker, Carlos. *Ernest Hemingway: A Life Story.* New York: Charles Scribner's Sons, 1969.

Baker, Carlos, Ed. *Ernest Hemingway: Selected Letters, 1917-1961.* New York: Scribner's, 1981.

Bellavance-Johnson, Marsha. *Hemingway in Key West.* Ketchum, Idaho: Computer Lab, 1987.

Brian, Denis. *The True Gen: An Intimate Portrait of Hemingway by Those Who Knew Him.* New York: Dell Publishing, 1988.

Davis, Elmer. "New World Symphony," *Harpers Magazine, May, 1935.*

Day, Jane. "Bimini, Bahamas: Hemingway's Island in the Stream," *South Florida History Magazine,* Fall, 1989.

de Groot, John. *Papa.* Boise, Idaho: Hemingway Western Studies Center, 1989.

de Groot, John. "A Farewell to Papa," *Sunshine Magazine,* January 6, 1984.

Dos Passos, John. *The Best Times.* New York: New American Library, 1966.

Dos Passos, John. "Old Hem Was a Sport," *Sports Illustrated,* June 29, 1964.

Heidelberg, Paul. "Boxer Hemingway Laced His Punches With Tips to His Sparring Partners," *Sports Illustrated,* December 23-30, 1985.

Hemingway, Gregory H. *Papa: A Personal Memoir.* Boston: Houghton Mifflin, 1976.

Hemingway, Leicester. *My Brother, Ernest Hemingway.* Cleveland: World, 1961.

Hemingway, Lorian. "Leicester: The Other Hemingway," *Clockwatch Review,* Vol. III, No. 2, 1986.

Kaufelt, Lynn Mitsuko. *Key West Writers and Their Houses.* Sarasota: Pineapple Press/Omnigraphics, 1986.

Kert, Bernice. *The Hemingway Women.* New York: Norton, 1983.

Klingener, Nancy. "The Importance of Selling Ernest," *The Miami Herald,* July 22, 1992.

Langley, Joan and Wright. *Key West: Images of the Past.* Key West: C.C. Belland and E.O. Swift, 1982.

BIBLIOGRAPHY CONTINUED

Langley, Wright and Windhorn, Stan. *Yesterday's Key West.* Miami: Seemann Publishing, 1973.

Lynn, Kenneth S. *Hemingway.* New York: Ballantine, 1987.

McLendon, James. *Papa: Hemingway in Key West.* Key West: Langley Press, 1990.

Putney, Michael. "Key West: Papa Still Remembered," *The National Observer*, August 23, 1975.

Rovere, Richard R. "End of the Line," *The New Yorker*, December 15, 1951.

Wells, Sharon. *Sloppy Joe's Bar: The First Fifty Years.* Key West: Key West Saloon, 1983.

White, William, Editor. *By-Line: Ernest Hemingway.* New York: Scribner's, 1967.

INDEX

Numbers in italics refer to illustrations.